MW01612550

## NOTES ON

# ROMANS 1–8

### BOOK ONE
Chapters 1–3: The Problem We All Have

## BILL SPENCER

## – NARROW GATE –

Narrow Gate Foundation
P.O. Box 267
Duck River, TN 38454

ISBN: 979-8-9868505-8-0

Printed in Canada

# Table of Contents

# Foreword

**W**hy? I suppose that's a good question to begin with. Generations of theologians have written innumerable books containing invaluable insights into the mysteries of Scripture. Why would anyone want to pick up this little book? It's not the work of an accredited theologian who has spent a lifetime in the halls of academia gleaning wisdom and insight from heralded scholars. So, "Why" seems to be a fair question. Unfortunately, the answer isn't really all that remarkable.

For starters, thoughts move in and out of my head fast enough that if I don't write them down, I'll forget them (maybe you can relate). So, I take notes. To be fair, I rarely go back and study those notes. Sure, I refer to them from time to time, but I don't really study them, as if I'm preparing for an exam. I was always terrible at that sort of thing anyway. But I find that if I take notes and organize my thoughts while working through Scripture, the picture of my conversation with God becomes clearer. If I simply read and think, my mind drifts, and I rarely come to any clarified understanding that I can share with someone else. And isn't that the point of studying Scripture? To ingest something so deeply that its existence within you to not only nourishes you but also gives you something to pass along to others?

The title of this book is fairly accurate. Not *The Mysteries Revealed* or *A Theological Commentary*. Instead, this is just a book of notes from one person who decided to write down what he saw as he studied his way through the text. But that still doesn't fully answer the question of why you are holding this book.

This book is far more than a record of my notes or thoughts. As you leaf through the pages, you'll notice that many of them are lined but not filled, and they have the heading "My Notes." These pages are the reasons why you're holding this book. Those pages are for you.

The notes contained in the book aren't designed to share insights that can't easily be found in multiple study resources. Rather, they are designed to get you to think and talk with God about His timeless and perfect expression of love toward you. The lined pages are interspersed with the populated ones, so you can record your notes. That's really the point of this exercise. It's not for you to learn what someone else thinks or knows; it's for you to record what you think and know. The notes are simply a primer for conversations between you and God. And that conversation is what truly matters.

As you record your thoughts, observations, insights, questions, and answers, you'll begin to connect more deeply with the text than you ever have before. And as you discover things for yourself, you'll have something to share with the people you encounter. That's the purpose of this book. You'll probably even notice, as you read through the pages that follow, that the recorded notes sound more like a discussion than observations. That's because I use my notes as a space where I can exercise how I'll share the insights of my study with the people I'll encounter. I'm not suggesting you should do the same, but it's a good practice that has served me well for several years.

At Narrow Gate, where I spend the majority of my time, we're fond of saying, "Discovered truth is always more powerful than delivered truth." Here's your chance to discover truth that you can carry in your soul and share with others for the rest of your life. Here's a chance for the words and thoughts of God to become your words and thoughts. When that happens, you'll begin to notice how the words of God migrate into your daily conversations. You'll find yourself discovering how the struggles of life from thousands of years in the past are still present with us today. You'll build a compass of unchanging truth that will help you navigate the journey of our days from now until we see God face to face.

In short, if you'll take the time to compile your notes—your conversations with God about His timeless truth—you'll be changed into a vessel of loving compassion that can be used to rescue and transform others. And that is a good answer to the question, "Why?"

So, let's get started.

# Introduction

Luke was a quiet student. He didn't talk as much as the other students in his class, but when he did speak, it was always honest. And by "honest," I don't mean that he simply told the truth—although he certainly did that. What I mean is that there was a transparent sincerity about every question and every response that came out of his mouth. Luke wasn't the kind of guy given to jokes or sarcasm like a lot of the students at Narrow Gate Lodge. When he had a genuine question, he genuinely asked it. When he had a response to something we were discussing, he offered that response without much of a social filter. And if you asked Luke a question, he would answer as truthfully as he could. He didn't try to tell you what you wanted to hear, and he never offered the answer that would just cause the moment to pass by without interrupting the flow of the conversation.

To be honest, it wasn't something I was accustomed to. After working with hundreds of Narrow Gate students, I had developed a skeptical ear when listening to responses—always wondering if the answer was coming from a place of real belief and conviction, or if it was simply a tactic to escape a conversation that might take some time because it uncovered a position in life that needed work.

This night was no exception. And although I knew Luke to be a quietly honest guy who answered every question with integrity and transparency, I still didn't expect the answer that came from my simple question. Let me explain, but I'll have to provide further information for you to know just how abruptly a two-word answer changed the course of teaching and learning at Narrow Gate Lodge.

Days at Narrow Gate Lodge are fairly predictable. Students begin their day at 7:00 with a self-led study and a cup of coffee. Breakfast at 8:00 is followed by a staff-led Bible study at 9:00. At 10:30 there's an exercise break—usually filled with a spirited game of ultimate frisbee. Lunch is served at noon. From 1:00 to 5:00 is filled with work on the property or in the creative shops, and dinner is served at 6:00. Free time and phone calls last until 7:30. Then we roll into "Late Night."

Late Night is another hour and a half of study and discussion, and it happens to be my favorite segment of the day. It's a bit more free-form and conversational than the rest of the day, and that lends itself to a much higher level of interaction than any one of our standard curriculum pieces. The night I'm speaking of was no exception.

I had planned on having a discussion with the guys regarding the crowns that are listed in the Bible as rewards for those who have offered their lives to Jesus in the trust that He will save them. It's an interesting conversation because it goes beyond the normal thought of salvation being our "ticket" into heaven and starts a conversation about what things might be like once we get there. It's really supposed to be more thought provoking than anything else, but it still tends to spark some great conversation.

I was somewhere in the beginning of that discussion with the students when I decided to go around the room and ask the simple, qualifying question, "Are you going to heaven?" There may have been a dozen or fifteen guys in the room that night, and I started at one side and asked each of them individually, "Are you going to heaven?" One by one, each student answered confidently, "Yes." That is, until I reached

Luke. He was toward the end of the line, and when I pointed to him and asked, "Are you going to heaven?" he shrugged his shoulders and answered, "We'll see." And there it was: the two-word answer that completely derailed the planned conversation.

At this point in the progression of the Narrow Gate Lodge program, the issue of salvation was supposed to have been put to bed. This Late Night study was being taught to a group of students who had already worked their way through the Gospel of John, as well as our Narrow Gate curriculum entitled *Foundations of Faith*—both of which are designed to show that Jesus (who is God) had done everything necessary to make us acceptable to God. But despite the fact that Luke had been through those courses and received that information like every other student in his class, he didn't feel he could say "yes" with confidence, so he didn't.

His answer caught me off guard. The question was intended to be almost rhetorical, and I only wanted to ask it to establish the next question in my mind, which was supposed to focus on whether we want to maximize the experience of eternity by making wise spiritual investments during our time on earth. But it's difficult to move forward with a discussion about how we maximize our heavenly experience when the issue of our eternal security is still unsettled.

So in true Narrow Gate fashion, we set aside the planned study and started a new discussion to rehearse the truths of salvation that had been taught during the first weeks of a student's experience at Narrow Gate Lodge. But it became obvious that Luke needed a fresh perspective on the gospel of Jesus if he was going to become settled on the issue of whether he could be confident of his place in eternity. As I thought through which direction to take the study, I settled on a discussion through the first eight chapters of the book of Romans for a lot of reasons.

First, Luke was trying to settle an argument in his head that he believed had valid points on both sides. As he introduced his conundrum of faith versus works, I saw other students join him in his doubt. At its core, Luke's argument was similar to one that many people have when they compare their behavior in life to the perfect standard that is established in God's instruction for how we should live. It can be phrased in the question, "If I am saved, why don't I consistently refuse the temptation to sin? Isn't ongoing sin in my life an indicator that I'm not actually saved? I know that the Bible says that my faith in Christ will save me, but Jesus also said that if we love Him, we'll do what He commanded us to do."

As I listened to the discussion that ensued, I considered the merits of various studies that we could pursue to settle the minds and hearts of the guys in the room. I remembered that a review of the book of Romans was taught at Harvard Law for its first 100 years of existence as a primer to courtroom argumentation. The argument that the apostle Paul made regarding our salvation by faith was so sound that it became a model for how all debate can or should be constructed. And settling an internal, theological argument was exactly what we needed to do.

Second, while Romans 1–8 can be thought of as "The Gospel According to Paul," it does not follow the same format as the synoptic Gospels of Matthew, Mark, and Luke. Nor does it follow the symbolic structure of John. It's much more western in its approach to the telling of Jesus' purpose on earth. The basis for this type of inescapable logic is called *syllogism*, and it is probably the most palatable approach to western thinkers like us.

If you're unfamiliar with the term *syllogism*, it's a pattern of logical thinking that's constructed as: Predicate. Predicate. Conclusion. In other words, you have a grounded fact, followed by another grounded fact, that leads to a logical conclusion. That conclusion becomes a new grounded fact (predicate) that can be inserted into the next iteration of your thinking. The predicates can't be ambiguous, untrue, or illogical. If you want an example of how this works, think of the mathematical statement, "A=B, and B=C, therefore A=C." This is the basis for all philosophy. And Paul used it masterfully in his telling of the fall and rescue of mankind.

Third, I believe that one of our responsibilities as teachers at Narrow Gate is to give the students a reliable format that they can use to convey the truth of God's Word as they graduate into their commitment to serve the world. One of the mechanisms that we use to accomplish that goal is a chapter-by-chapter summation of the books we study. If we can help each student know the primary theme, instruction, or happening for each chapter we work through, they can recall that information in the midst of a conversation and go to that chapter of the text to help someone else see the beauty of God's loving offer of rescue. I know of no section of the text that divides into summary thoughts as effectively as Paul's telling of the gospel in Romans 1–8.

Luke needed a way to be sure that he was saved. He couldn't move forward in life and become the man he was called to be if we didn't resolve this issue. And I thought it would be beneficial if all the students of Narrow Gate Lodge had a clear understanding of Paul's telling of the gospel in the letter to the Romans so that they could use this logical and philosophical presentation to the people they would encounter throughout life.

So, I did what I typically do when I set out to study some portion of biblical text: I copied the first eight chapters of the book of Romans into a Word document, and I began to capture my thoughts *in-line* with the text. If you have the *Narrow Gate Notes on Ruth* or *Luke 15*, you already know what this process looks like. If this is your first rehearsal of the text through a *Narrow Gate Notes* book, I pray that you'll welcome the opportunity to have a conversation with God about your thoughts as you work your way through the pages ahead.

Don't rush. This book (Romans) is a complex syllogism, so each building block of logic needs to be well-grounded before we move on to the next segment of the conversation. Paul doesn't start with the glorious arrival of God on earth like the other Gospel writers. Instead, he draws the dark and hopeless background of man's separation from the Creator before introducing God's plan for brilliant, hopeful rescue. Having a deep understanding of the desperate position of a soul separated from God will only serve to amplify the gratitude we have for the costly rescue He chose to enact.

I'll say it again, *don't rush*. As you work your way through the language that the Holy Spirit uses in the writing of Paul, allow God to draw some new or deeper understanding of just how hopeless our position was before the singular and overpowering hope of Jesus was introduced into our story. Then, allow that dark and desperate understanding to give way to a grateful and hopeful joy as we join with Paul in saying,

> "I am persuaded that neither death nor life, nor angels nor principalities nor powers, nor things present nor things to come, nor height nor depth, nor any other created thing, shall be able to separate us from the love of God which is in Christ Jesus our Lord" (Romans 8:38–39).

CHAPTER 1

# Paul Declared Himself a Servant, and Christ, the Lord

**Romans 1:1** | "Paul, a bondservant of Jesus Christ, called to be an apostle, separated to the gospel of God."

**P**aul's letter to the Romans is widely considered one of the greatest treasures of philosophy ever written. Its richness is deeper than an individual can fathom in a lifetime. We would be foolish to think that this exercise will uncover all the depth of this letter. So, let's set a realistic expectation from the very start of our journey: The hope of this study is to spend time with God as He allows us to see some things that are new, or to expand what we already know into deeper and richer understanding.

As you read, if you feel the urge to go deeper, follow that urge. There are endless resources to help you explore the treasures of Romans. But these pages are only designed to get the conversation between you and God started. Few things will ground you in your faith like understanding this letter to the Roman church.

Martin Luther believed so deeply in the book of Romans that he wrote in the introduction to his *Lectures on Romans*: "This letter is truly the most important piece in the New Testament. It is purest Gospel. It is well worth a Christian's while not only to memorize it word for word but also to occupy himself with it daily, as though it were the daily bread of the soul. It is impossible to read or to meditate on this letter too much or too well. The more one deals with it, the more precious it becomes and the better it tastes."[1]

Knowing the impact it had on a man like Luther, I think it's well worth our time to pause and consider each verse with intention, asking what the Holy Spirit might want to plant in our hearts as we work our way through this gospel presentation.

So, we begin with a simple salutation from Paul. He typically used a couple of recurring descriptions in the opening lines of his letters—either "apostle" or "bondservant." Here, he used both. Paul was making two quick statements that are worth our attention: First, he recognized that his life is the possession of Jesus Christ (bondservant), and second, that this commitment to service had come with an appointment to the office of apostle.

An apostle carries great authority in the church; a bondservant carries none. The paradox of those two positions is intentional. Paul was saying that in himself he was nothing. But in Christ, he was the authoritative voice of instruction.

Let's take a closer look at these terms. *Bondservant*: If a man became the servant of another because of an unpayable debt, he was obligated to serve for as much as forty-nine years, depending on the size of the debt. However, every 50th year in the Hebrew calendar was the year of Jubilee, when every captive was to be released from his service to the master.

But a servant could choose not to leave. He might decide that he was better off in the service of the master than on his own. If so, the master would bore a hole in the servant's ear and place an earring in it to signify that the man was now a servant by choice—a bondservant. And that arrangement was permanent.

That's the declaration Paul made here. His life was not a debt being worked off; it was a free choice to serve the master who is Jesus.

Now, the word *apostle*. The *Strong's Concordance* defines the Greek word *apóstolos* as a delegate, specifically, an ambassador of the gospel, or one commissioned directly by Christ. The apostles were the ones charged to establish the church on earth. While some in modern society use the title liberally, the church has historically recognized that twelve men were personally chosen by Jesus to serve as apostles in this foundational role.

Finally, the word *gospel*. Literally, this word means "good news," but it carries a richer, more specific meaning. In ancient wars, when battles were fought far from the king's eye, a messenger would bring word of the outcome. If it was a victory, it was called a "gospel" message. The Greek word is *euangelion*, which is where we get our word *evangelism*. Paul was saying he had been charged with proclaiming the good news of victory in battle—a battle most people don't even realize is being waged against them by an enemy who wants to see them separated from the God who made them and loves them.

It's hard for us to accept that life as a servant can be better than life as a master. But when you're the master of a life filled with chaos and futility (see Romans 8:20), life is miserable—even if you're numb to it. When you serve a King of peace and light, life is wonderful, because you serve a Lord who provides hope of a good outcome, despite present circumstances.

In Romans 1:1, Paul declared himself to be a willfully, contented servant whose mission is to proclaim victory in war to a special people, in a special place, at a special time. Or, in Narrow Gate terms, Paul declared that he knew who he was and why he was here. Identity controls behavior. Purpose provides meaning in life.

Before we move on, let's address one more word: *called*. The idea of being called is as old as Scripture itself. The Hebrew word *vayikra*, meaning "called," is found repeatedly in the book of Leviticus. God's calling is a beckoning invitation. Paul was stating that God had invited him to the station of apostle, but like all of God's invitations, it came with clear parameters.

In Leviticus, God calls to Moses from the Tabernacle of Meeting, a picture of Jesus. Then He speaks to Moses, saying, "When any one of you brings an offering to the LORD, you shall bring your offering of the livestock—of the herd and of the flock" (1:2). In other words, anyone responding to God's call had to bring a life under their control. And the only life we truly control is our own. Paul will later say, we are to "present [ourselves] a living sacrifice" (Romans 12:1, emphasis added). Answering God's call is to offer our lives to Him in willing service—the very thing Jesus did for us.

Paul referred to us being "called" again in Romans 1:6,7, but in those instances he spoke to the whole church, saying that we also have received the same invitation to be saints of God. Without that call, we could not have salvation. Paul's message is clear from the start and will be repeated: God is responsible for our entire salvation.

One last observation before we move on. I love that Paul said he was "separated" by the gospel (v. 1). We won't speculate on all the things he's separated from—there are too many paths to chase. But let

me offer one thought to ponder: We live in a society obsessed with individuality. We tell our kids they can be anything they want to be, but that's not entirely true. Worse, if we become the autonomous determiners of our course, we remove God from His rightful seat.

Paul tackled this in depth later, but I'll propose here that we only become what we're truly intended to be when we hand the pen of our life story over to God and let Him write it. He is life, liberty, and the source of joy that far surpasses happiness.

If anyone ever suggests that submission to God robs us of our unique voice, they've missed the heart of the gospel. Paul made it clear: What set him apart and made him who he was always intended to be is this gospel of which he is not ashamed (v. 16–17). To be separated from something is always to be separated to something. And nothing allows us to find our truest, most unique voice like the gospel of Christ, which enlivens and empowers our voice of hope and love to a world desperate for both.

> **Romans 1:2 |** "Which He promised before through His prophets in the Holy Scriptures."

There is a common phrase that many of us have heard: "The New Testament is in the Old Testament concealed. And the Old Testament is in the New Testament revealed." That phrase is applicable here as Paul made a simple observation that has profound implications in our studies throughout our lives.

I've been a part of many worship traditions in my life—some liturgical, some evangelical, and some charismatic. I find beauty and value in all of them. But they all have varying views on the value and purpose of

the Old Testament writings. So, I think it's important to consider what Jesus said about the Scriptures that He learned growing up.

One of the earliest examples we have for consideration is found in Luke 4, when Jesus read from the scroll of Isaiah; in our Bible it would be Isaiah 61:1-2. Luke's account says this, "He unrolled the scroll and found the place where it was written, 'The Spirit of the Lord is upon me, because he has anointed me to proclaim good news to the poor. He has sent me to proclaim liberty to the captives and recovering of sight to the blind, to set at liberty those who are oppressed, to proclaim the year of the Lord's favor.' And he rolled up the scroll and gave it back to the attendant and sat down. And the eyes of all in the synagogue were fixed on him. And he began to say to them, 'Today this Scripture has been fulfilled in your hearing'" (Luke 4:17-21, ESV).

In that moment, Jesus was making it clear that one of the purposes for Isaiah's writings, which had been penned some 750 years earlier, was to forecast—or "prophesy"—the coming King of Israel. I would doubt the people in the synagogue that day had any other viewpoint of Jesus' claims, "Today this scripture has been fulfilled in your hearing" (v. 21), was Him saying, "I am Messiah, the promised King of Israel." They were so furious with His statement and claim, they drove Him out of the town to the edge of a cliff with the intention of killing Him.

This is just one example of Jesus' claim that the Tanach (which is the Hebrew word for *Bible*) was a repeated and detailed picture of Him. In John 5:39, Jesus told a group of Jewish rulers, "You search the Scriptures because you think that in them you have eternal life; and it is they that bear witness about me" (ESV). Again in Luke 24, Jesus is talking with a couple of guys who were returning home after the catastrophic Passover feast in which He had been crucified. The two men didn't

recognize Jesus, so they were lamenting to Him about how they had hoped that this Man was, "a prophet mighty in deed and word before God and all the people" (v. 19, ESV). He would be "the one to redeem Israel" (v. 21, ESV). Jesus listened to what they had to say and then responded with an explanation and some evidence that we would do well to pay attention to. Luke records the conversation this way: "And he said to them, 'O foolish ones, and slow of heart to believe all that the prophets have spoken! Was it not necessary that the Christ should suffer these things and enter into his glory?' And beginning with Moses and all the Prophets, he interpreted to them in all the Scriptures the things concerning himself" (Luke 24:25–27, ESV)

Here's the point I'm driving at: Jesus told the Jewish worshippers that Isaiah's writings had prophesied His arrival. He told the ruling Jewish elite that they worked their way through Scripture thinking that its instructions were designed to offer them eternal life. But they were missing the fact that *He is* eternal life, and those same Scriptures were a testimony and description of Him. Then He showed the guys returning to Emmaus that *all* of their Scripture pertains to Him. So, if we read the Old Testament Scriptures looking for specific instructions on how *we* should live *our lives*, we miss the more mature purpose of those writings, which is to show us who and how God is. Jesus is the human manifestation of the living God, and to know Him is to know God.

Most people read the Bible stories in the Old Testament as if they are intended to tell us how to "live our lives." I'll have to agree that there is some element of truth in that thinking. However, the problem with that line of thought is it makes the "living" of "our lives" up to us. If we have truly been crucified with Christ, and it is actually His life being lived through our daily experience, then we must give a great deal of

consideration to the idea that Christianity is more about Jesus living His life through us and less about us living our lives for Him. Somewhere in the cooperative balance of these two thoughts, we can find the pathway that leads to the life that God has providentially designed for us to live.

I see David's bravery in the face of Goliath, and I can infer that the story is teaching me to be brave in the face of God's enemies. And that is just one of a thousand stories with a thousand outcomes where I can choose to believe that the Bible is designed to teach me how to live my life. But if you look at the opening of verse 3 in this study of Romans, you'll see something very interesting that can change that perspective. Paul said that the promise of God, that came through the prophets and the Holy Scriptures, is the promise concerning Jesus. If you allow Scripture to take on that light, you'll see a different story altogether. You won't see David facing Goliath or you facing your giants. You'll see Jesus defeating Satan using the very weapon formed to prosper against Him. And while both perspectives are true, one keeps us as the primary focal point, while the other keeps Jesus as the primary point of consideration.

The Old Testament does ultimately reveal how our lives are to be lived. Yet, I'm not sure that its instruction is exactly the way many of us perceive it at first glance. The number of passages in the New Testament that support the idea that Christ's life is to be manifested through us is overwhelming. To complement that, the Old Testament is a perfectly woven tapestry of repeated revelations about who and how God is. And, therefore, who and how Jesus is. The Tabernacle of Exodus is a picture of Jesus. The outline of Leviticus is a beautiful picture that points to His atonement for our sin. The whole book of Isaiah

screams of His coming life. And the more I study, the more I believe that every passage of Scripture holds some thread of revelation about Jesus' life.

We are to live submitted to Christ so that He can then live His life through us. And the more we know Him, the more that becomes possible. We should look for Him in every verse we read. Understanding how much He loves us will cause change in your life that doesn't even require "conscious" thought. As the old song says, "Turn your eyes upon Jesus. Look full in His wonderful face. And the things of earth will grow strangely dim, in the light of His glory and grace."

Even the most blatant passages of scriptural command can be seen in this light. Consider the ten commandments listed in Exodus 20 or Deuteronomy 5. They not only give us instruction for what our lives will look like if we are totally submitted to God, it can serve the dual purpose of revealing the character and nature of God by compelling us to live as He is. God doesn't murder, so we shouldn't either. He doesn't covet or steal or lie, and He is never unfaithful. And if we truly want to express our love for Him, we should strive to be like Him by avoiding theft and envy and dishonesty. Fidelity to God is the standard because He is always faithful toward us.

But we all know that we don't live up to the standard. That's why Paul took the time to pen this letter to the Roman church. He's providing a balance to the conundrum that lives inside of each of us by explaining exactly how God deals with our shortcomings. And, in so doing, Paul exposes us to the truth of how just and merciful our Father truly is.

I feel like I'm getting way ahead of myself here. So, let's get back to the study. But please keep in mind that Paul was establishing the fact that the Hebrew Bible is a giant, screaming declaration that God has

always had a loving plan to overcome our shortcomings—and that plan is Jesus' sacrifice on our behalf. When Jesus died in our place, it's as if we died and paid the required price for the less-than-perfect lives that we all lived. Paul made the argument that all we have to do is trust in God's loving provision through the life, death, burial, and resurrection of Jesus.

Ok, let's keep moving.

> **Romans 1:3 |** "Concerning His Son Jesus Christ our Lord, who was born of the seed of David according to the flesh."

"Born according to the flesh" simply refers to the fact that Jesus' physical lineage is traceable to King David, as promised in Scripture. His spiritual lineage is God the Father through the work of the Holy Spirit. But His earthly, physical lineage came from the line of David.

So, why did Jesus have human lineage? The writer of the book of Hebrews said that Jesus can sympathize with our plight because He was tempted just as we are tempted (4:15)? Without Jesus' human lineage, we could have looked at Him and said, "You simply don't know what it's like." God went to elaborate lengths to prove a point to us that we would be irresponsible to ignore. In God's unending mercy, He declared, "I cannot remove you from the suffering life that you have chosen, but I can join you in that suffering."

God limited Himself (in Christ) to a human experience so that He could empathize with every single human ailment that we are subjected to. Jesus was a man, dependent on the power of the Holy Spirit just as we are. Jesus knew hunger, pain, joy, and curiosity just as we do.

More importantly, Jesus knew what it was to be *totally* dependent upon another for life and guidance. He experienced all of that because

God chose to have a human lineage, as well as a spiritual purity. By joining us fully in our humanity, Jesus removed any opportunity to claim that He could not understand us. He walked in our shoes, breathed our air, suffered our suffering—all to prove that His rescue was both personal and complete.

> **Romans 1:4 |** "And declared to be the Son of God with power according to the Spirit of holiness, by the resurrection from the dead."

What single thing can you point to that truly and uniquely declares the "Godhood" of Jesus? It's simple and profound: He was resurrected from the dead! Gandhi, Mohammed, Confucius, Joseph Smith, and every other religious or philosophical leader died and was buried. They are still in that state to this very day. *Only* Jesus came out of the grave with a resurrected body that would never see decay again.

Someone might respond, "What about Lazarus? He was raised from the dead by Jesus." And you'd be correct; he was raised from the dead. But Lazarus returned to the same mortal state in which he existed before his passing. The difference is that when Jesus was raised from the dead, He wasn't simply resuscitated; He was resurrected! Lazarus went on to live for some time and then died again. But Jesus never died again. There is coming a day, as 1 John 3:2 reminds us, when we will be "like Him," and we too will never die.

So, when someone wants to claim that Jesus is just one of several ways to God, just ask them: "Which of those *other ways* was resurrected from the dead by the power of the Spirit?" This is no small distinction. Make sure you can speak to the validity of the Scriptures and be ready to walk people through the account of Jesus' death, burial,

and resurrection. This is unique to the Christian faith. It is unique to all of existence because it is uniquely God. Only Jesus was willing to live the life that we are born into—with all of its temptation and difficulty—and then choose to suffer and die to display the depth of His love for us.

Let's not skip past an equally critical point. In order for Jesus to be raised from the dead, He first had to experience death. And the death He experienced was coupled with suffering and humiliation. Religion commonly supports a worldview that claims the goal of life is to avoid or escape suffering. Jesus teaches us something radically different.

In the Christian worldview, the goal is to experience sympathy, compassion, and joy (yes, joy) amid our suffering. Please don't rush by this statement without letting it sink into your soul. If you allow it, this truth can change you—deeply, eternally, and practically. This is the life Jesus modeled for us, and it is the life He desires to live through us.

**Romans 1:5** | "Through Him we have received grace and apostleship for obedience to the faith among all nations for His name."

I've lost count of the number of encouraging responses I've received from people who've worked their way through these little books. They've shared how these notes have sparked conversations with their kids around the dinner table, opened up great discussions in small group Bible studies, or simply helped them see God's Word from a perspective they had never considered before. I always love hearing those stories. But if I'm honest, when I bump into a verse like this one, I can't help but wonder if anything I write will ever come close to doing justice to the depth that's packed into just these few words.

It's not that I don't want to record my thoughts or create something that might help spark reflection in someone else's soul. It's more that I know, deep down, that my little observations are so limited—so inadequate—when I'm staring at a verse as loaded as this verse. But since this format only gives us a few paragraphs to work with, we'll do the best we can and trust the Holy Spirit to fill in the gaps as He walks with you through this conversation.

Let's start with the idea that maybe we need to expand our understanding of grace a bit. I've heard it taught more times than I can count that grace is the "unmerited favor of God." And honestly, that's a solid definition in most cases. There are a lot of times where that definition fits beautifully, where grace is clearly God's merciful act of loving us even when we don't deserve it. And I never want to minimize or dismiss that view of grace. It's true, and it's precious.

But if we're being honest—and we need to be—there are some moments in Scripture where that simple definition feels like it doesn't quite capture the whole picture. Could it be that grace is even more than unmerited favor? I think so. In fact, I think the Bible teaches that. James Ryle did a teaching series years ago titled *Amazing Grace*, and if you ever want to dive deeper into the heart of this, I can't recommend it enough. He asks some tough questions and answers them with a clarity that sticks with you. I won't try to duplicate his work here, but I do want to share some of his insights that have reshaped how I think about grace.

James described grace like this: "The empowering presence of God that enables me to be all I was intended to be and do all I was intended to do." That hits me hard every time I hear it. If you adopt that understanding, a lot of things in Scripture that might have seemed like

contradictions or paradoxes start to make a lot more sense. Let me give you two quick examples.

First: Galatians 5:4 says, "You who would be justified by the law; you have fallen away from grace" (ESV). Now if grace is unmerited favor, why would it be given to us when we didn't deserve it, but then be taken away when we act in a way that shows we still don't deserve it? That doesn't seem to add up. Wouldn't you think that if grace is for the undeserving, then the more undeserving we act, the more grace would flow? Is Paul saying that we're saved by grace at the start, but then we lose it if we try to earn it? That would be a mess.

Let's be clear: Paul wasn't talking to people outside the faith. This letter is addressed to the "churches of Galatia" (1:1). These are believers. He opens the letter by saying, "Grace to you and peace from God our Father and the Lord Jesus Christ, who gave Himself for our sins to deliver us from the present evil age" (1:3–4). So, there's no doubt he's writing to individuals who had already experienced saving grace. Yet, he warns them that they can fall away from grace. Not from salvation necessarily, but from the empowering presence of God that enables them to walk in truth and freedom.

Paul even said later in that same chapter, "You ran well. Who hindered you from obeying the truth?" (5:7). That phrase, "falling away from grace" (v. 4), has to mean something more than just losing salvation. I believe it means they were trying to live the Christian life in their own strength, under their own power, by their own efforts—and that never works. Grace saves us and grace sanctifies us. It's God's empowering presence that enables both.

Second: James 4:6 says, "God resists the proud, But gives grace to the humble." Now, if grace is unmerited favor, why wouldn't God

pour it out on the proud, since they, by definition, deserve it the least? Why does He give it to the humble, who seem to be closer to the mark already? That's a hard one to explain unless we're willing to expand our definition of grace to include God's empowering presence. If grace is the strength of God flowing into our lives to do what we can't do on our own, then of course it makes sense that the humble receive it. They're the ones who know they need it. The proud are trying to handle life on their own terms. When we take the reins of control out of God's hands, He lets us. When we do that, His grace—that empowering presence— withdraws, and we're left with nothing but our own strength. That futility, in turn, drives us back to the foot of the cross in desperate surrender.

Grace flows from the posture Paul laid out at the start of this letter. He was nothing on his own, but when he surrendered to Christ, the power of the Holy Spirit turned him into an apostle. Grace comes from God through Christ, by the Spirit, and it's poured out on the humble who know they can't live the life God intends apart from His empowering presence. Grace saves us. Grace sanctifies us. Grace refines and matures us as Jesus' life becomes more and more visible in our own.

Let me offer one last thought before we move on: Paul said here that grace is what allows us to obey the faith. So many times, we fall into the trap of "trying harder" to live the Christian life, when it's the empowering presence of God through the finished work of Jesus that enables us to do anything at all that's pleasing to Him. That should humble us right down to our knees. Even our initial act of faith—the ability to trust God—is a gift of grace. It's God's empowering presence that allows belief to take root in our hearts. It's His ongoing flow of grace that grows that belief over time. And it's His grace that allows the life of Christ to shine brighter in us as we walk through the seasons of life.

Paul's going to dig into this a lot more in Chapter 5, but for now, I hope you'll let this truth sink deep into your heart. Let it foster some honest, grateful prayer where all you can say is, "Thank You, God, for grace."

**Romans 1:6** | "Among whom you also are the called of Jesus Christ."

Now here's a little line from Paul that I think we need to sit with for a minute before rushing on. Paul took a moment to position himself before his readers as a man fully rooted in Christ—a bondservant, an apostle, a man whose entire life is surrendered to the gospel of Jesus. But notice what he does next. He doesn't let the attention stay on himself for long. With a few simple words, he turns the spotlight and reminds his readers that they, too, are equal inheritors in this promise of Christ.

He says they are also "the called of Jesus Christ." I'll tell you: That's not a throwaway phrase. That's us. I can't count the number of sermons I've heard over the years that focus on the sinfulness of man—and don't get me wrong, those messages aren't wrong. We are sinners. Paul's going to make that crystal clear in just a few verses. But if we stop there—if we let "sinner" become the defining statement of who we are—we miss something critical. In fact, I'd go so far as to say that if we live with "sinner" as our primary identity, all we'll do is perpetuate more sin in our lives.

Identity has a way of driving behavior. Paul wasn't shy about establishing identity right out of the gate. He's writing to the saints in Rome—the "called of Christ." And I believe those types of affirming truths are the bedrock of hope in our lives. When we start to see ourselves the way God sees us, when we begin to accept that we've been made holy

and set apart through the sacrifice and resurrection of Jesus, something inside us starts to shift. We start to act like the saints we already are.

I've said this before, and I'll keep saying it because it's just that important: Your understanding of your identity will shape the way you live your life. That's why we've created two entire books on the subject: *Narrow Gate Notes on Identity* and *Narrow Gate Notes on Purpose.* If you've never walked through those books, I'd highly recommend them. These two books have been core curriculum at Narrow Gate Lodge for as long as I can remember, and they've helped countless people walk into the freedom that comes when you finally let your identity flow from what God says about you instead of what the world—or your own brokenness—tries to convince you of. They'll help you unpack the truth of who you are in Christ, and why you're here on this earth. And if you've already been through them, maybe this is a good moment to circle back and let those truths sink in even deeper.

Paul continued building on this theme as we move through the next few verses, so let's keep reading and see where he takes us.

## The Church Is Loved by God and Possesses the Same Calling as Paul

**Romans 1:7 |** "To all who are in Rome, beloved of God, called to be saints: Grace to you and peace from God our Father and the Lord Jesus Christ."

It's worth noting that the way Paul opened this letter is a bit different from the way he begins most of his other letters, or to use the more scholarly term, epistles. Here he gives an unusually extended

introduction of himself before he even gets to his formal greeting or the heart of his message. There's probably a good reason for that. Unlike his other letters, Paul had never personally visited the church in Rome. As we'll see in the verses ahead, Paul wanted to go to Rome for some time but was prevented from doing so. So, he was writing this letter not as a personal follow-up to his previous visits, but as a way of laying a clear and unified foundation for the church's understanding of the gospel of Jesus Christ.

He began by establishing his own identity in Christ—as a bondservant and an apostle. Then he clarified Christ's identity as the Son of God and Lord of lords. Now, right here in this verse, he spoke directly to the Roman believers, offering them a reminder of their own identity.

When put together these three things create a foundation that's hard to shake: the authority of the gospel writer, the undeniable nature of Jesus, and the inherited identity and calling of every believer. It's a powerful combination, and one worth slowing down to consider. When we know what we're reading is the inspired truth of God (written through the vessel of Paul, declaring the incarnate deity of Jesus Christ, who has the authority to name us and place us into His service), well, that kind of knowledge will stabilize our faith and give clarity to our purpose. I know that's a mouthful, but it's worth reading again.

While we're here, let's pause long enough to notice the two descriptive phrases Paul used to define the recipients of this letter. He called them "saints" and the "beloved of God." I'll be honest, I think a lot of us struggle to see ourselves that way. We've grown up in a culture—and, frankly, in church traditions—that reserve the term "saint" for a special class of believers. People we imagine lived lives of extraordinary holiness, or who were somehow qualified for the title by the church

itself. And while I'm not here to criticize those traditions, I will point out something you can't miss in this text: Paul was addressing the entire church in Rome. He didn't separate them into the common folks and the spiritual elite. He didn't use the title "saint" sparingly. He gave it to the whole congregation.

And that raises a question for us: Is that how you see yourself? When you look in the mirror, do you see a beloved saint of God? Or do you see yourself through the lens of your behavior, your shortcomings, your habits, your struggles? Do you let those things define you? Because here's the truth that Paul laid down from the opening lines of this letter: If you are in Christ, then your identity is saint. You are beloved. And the quicker we begin to see ourselves through God's eyes, the sooner our behavior begins to match our true identity.

Yes, we still struggle with sin. Yes, we still trip over our own feet more often than we'd like to admit. And Paul will get to that. But don't miss this: Transformation begins when we agree with what God says about us. When we embrace our identity in Christ, our behavior begins to follow suit, not the other way around.

If this idea is new to you, or if you feel like you've heard it before but it never quite landed, I'd encourage you, as I mentioned before, to spend some time in *Narrow Gate Notes on Identity* and *Narrow Gate Notes on Purpose*.

As we continue moving through this letter, you'll notice that Paul kept coming back to this theme of contrast—the difference between light and dark, saint and sinner, freedom and bondage. He spent the next several chapters painting a pretty bleak picture of humanity's desperate condition apart from Christ. He wanted to make it painfully clear that we were all enslaved to sin at one point. We were all captives to its

power. But in chapter 6, he's made a bold declaration: We are no longer slaves to sin but have been made slaves to righteousness. We get to choose whose servants we will be.

If we can grasp that truth now—before Paul even gets to the heavy stuff—we'll be better prepared to understand that the evil that still trips us is an old influence we've grown far too accustomed to following. God's love and His sacrifice in Christ creates a new path for us. A way to escape not just the penalty of sin, but the persuasion of sin. And one day, even the very presence of sin.

So, before we move forward, let's just stop and sit with this for a moment. You, my friend, are a saint. You are beloved by God. And the sooner you embrace that truth, the sooner your life will begin to reflect it.

> **Romans 1:8 |** "First, I thank my God through Jesus Christ for you all, that your faith is spoken of throughout the whole world."

I have sons in the faith who travel the globe doing mission work. They are some of the most deeply loved people in my life, and I pray for them often. I can't fully express to you what it does to my heart when one of them returns home for a season of rest. When our eyes meet, everything else fades. I drop what I'm doing, move anything between us, and hug them with tears of gratitude running down my face. That embrace can last longer than what most people might call comfortable, but I don't care. The expression of love and joy in that moment must come first. It's not optional. It's necessary.

Paul did the same thing in this verse. Now that the introductions were behind him, he began the "body" of this letter with the word "First." In Greek, the word is *proton*, meaning "firstly" or "chiefly." It's a word of

priority. Paul was essentially saying, "Before I do anything else, before I go any further, you need to hear this." And what did he want them to hear? That he was grateful for them. That their faith had become famous, spoken of throughout the whole world. That's the kind of faith that inspires me to ask, "Lord, could You help me live a life that compels others to say the same about me?" I'd love to know that the first thing people think of when they think of me is, "That man walks by faith."

Maybe this is a good place to pause and do a little self-assessment. Is that how people would describe us? I'm not suggesting that faith somehow surpasses love. Not at all. But real faith in Christ is faith in love itself, because God is love, and Jesus is God. When we live out our faith, when our actions match what we say we believe, that kind of faith always shows up in sacrificial, selfless acts of love.

What would it look like if, in every conversation, the first thing out of our mouths was a word of encouragement—calling out the character of Christ we see in the person in front of us? Can you imagine what it would feel like if someone started his or her conversation with you by saying, "I need to tell you how much your joy lifts my spirit"? Or, "Your relentless commitment to keeping your promises challenges me to step up my own game"? What if we made it a practice to speak first to the Christlikeness we see in others? It might change not just their day, but their life.

> **Romans 1:9 |** "For God is my witness, whom I serve with my spirit in the gospel of His Son, that without ceasing I make mention of you always in my prayers."

Verses like this always give me a gut check. I read Paul's words, and I must ask myself, "Can I, like Paul, call God as my witness that I'm

praying faithfully for the people I love?" If I'm being honest, the answer is, "Not always." There are too many days where I let the tyranny of the urgent steal that time away from me.

I think part of the problem is that we all lean a little too much on our own abilities, especially when God has blessed us with talents and strengths. We get into the rhythm of doing things in our own power, and it's only when those abilities get blocked—when God takes away our capacity to fix, solve, or act—that we finally turn to Him and cry out, "Help!" And even then, if I'm honest, what I'm often really asking is for Him to help me accomplish the thing I want, rather than surrendering to the possibility that He might want to do something entirely different through me.

When we constantly credit God for any ability, any success, any outcome, our posture changes. We live in daily dependence. In that place we can, like Paul, call God as witness to the constancy of our prayer. Not just for the people we love, but for every aspect of our lives.

Paul tied that type of ongoing prayer directly to his love for the Roman believers. He said he mentions them "without ceasing." That phrase always used to trip me up. For years, I wrestled with what it could possibly mean to "pray without ceasing," like Paul said again in 1 Thessalonians 5:17. It felt like an impossible standard. After all, we sleep. We talk. We drive. We eat. We get distracted. At some point, the prayer must cease, right? And yes, I know that sounds ridiculous when you say it out loud, but that's where my head used to go.

That's when I discovered the beauty of tools like e-Sword (a free Bible study software you should investigate). I looked up different translations and found that the Complete Jewish Bible translates 1 Thessalonians 5:17 as, "Pray regularly." That made a lot more sense

to my practical mind. Commentators like John Gill and Albert Barnes helped, too. They explain that this isn't about literally living life on our knees while ignoring the rest of our responsibilities, but rather about continually returning to prayer with a spirit of joyful persistence.

Here's a mental image that's always stuck with me: Have you ever had the hiccups? I read about a guy named Charles Osborne who hiccupped for 68 years. Not every second of every day, but continually—over and over—for decades. That's what it means to pray without ceasing—a returning rhythm that never truly goes away.

Before we move on, I want to toss in one more angle on this whole idea of ceaseless prayer. I learned it from a man named Bill Gillham. I never got to meet him in person, but his books—*What God Wishes Christians Knew About Christianity* and *Lifetime Guarantee*—shaped my understanding of life in Christ more than almost anything else. Bill teaches that our souls communicate in two directions—physically through our bodies and spiritually through our spirits. That means I can be fully engaged in a conversation with you while, at the same time, carrying on an internal conversation with my heavenly Father. It's a skill. It takes time to grow into it, but once you start living that way, everything about your prayer life changes. If that's a new idea for you, I can't recommend Bill's books enough.

> **Romans 1:10 |** "Making request if, by some means, now at last I may find a way in the will of God to come to you."

I know we're taking our time here in chapter 1, but there are some foundational truths Paul laid down that are worth pausing over. They will shape the way we read everything that follows. And this verse right

here is one of those spots. Specifically, it's the little phrase tucked in there: "in the will of God."

In the original Greek, there are a couple of different ways to talk about God's will. The first is *thelesis*, which refers to God's unshakable, unstoppable, sovereign will. It's the kind of will that doesn't ask for permission. For example, Hebrews 2:4 uses this term when it describes God deciding to bear witness to His plan of salvation through signs, miracles, and wonders. No cooperation needed. God just does it.

But the word Paul used here is *thelema*, and that's different. It refers to God's desires; His will in the sense of what He would like to see happen, but which still requires our participation. Like 1 Thessalonians 4:3, where Paul wrote, "For this is the will of God, your sanctification." That's what God wants for us, but He's not going to force it on us. We must choose it.

Think of it like a man on one knee with an engagement ring. His desire is made clear, but the outcome still depends on the woman's response.

So, when Paul said he wanted to visit Rome but only if it was in the will of God, he was showing us what mature obedience looks like. He had a desire, but he was holding it loosely. In essence, he was saying, "I'll pursue it, but I won't bulldoze my way there if it's not what God wants." And if we live that way, it would change everything—our prayers, our conversations, even our decision-making process. What if we refused to move forward in anything until we first consulted God?

One last thought before we move on. The goal of life is not perfect obedience to God's will—at least not in the way we often think of it. If that were the goal, we'd all be doomed by now. No, the goal is to live in such communion with God that obedience becomes the natural fruit of a life surrendered to Him. It's not about gritting our teeth and forcing

compliance. It's about surrendering, listening, and walking in step with the One who loves us more than we can imagine.

> **Romans 1:11-12 |** "For I long to see you, that I may impart to you some spiritual gift, so that you may be established— that is, that I may be encouraged together with you by the mutual faith both of you and me."

There are a couple of thoughts here that deserve our attention. The first thought centers on Paul's statement that he desired to visit the church in Rome so that he might impart some spiritual gift. That statement is preceded by the fact that he actually "long(ed)" to see them.

I believe that Paul had a true longing in his heart to give something to the church in Rome that would solidify and advance their faith in Jesus. But it could be easy to fall into the trap of believing that this posture is reserved exclusively for believers who are mature in Christ, and that's simply not true. Let me explain.

There isn't a believer in history who wasn't endowed with certain gifts from the Holy Spirit. I'm not going to dive off into a rehearsal of Romans 12 and 1 Corinthians 12, where Paul begins to list those different types of gifts. I'll leave that for you to explore. But I do want to talk as if we've already settled the issue of gifts, which include service, encouragement, giving, and mercy, as well as prophecy, tongues, healing, and so forth. Then I want to continue to 1 Corinthians 13 and look at the fact that Paul elevated one gift above all others. He introduced that gift with the phrase, "I show you a more excellent way" (v. 31).

Love is the greatest gift that anyone can offer in this lifetime. It's love that compels sacrificial giving. It's love that drives every act of service or mercy. It's love (God is love. See 1 John 4:8-9.) that empowers

every prophecy and every miraculous healing that man has ever experienced. And it is love that compelled God to inhabit this world and rescue us from an inescapable destiny of separation from Him.

Love exists inside each of us, and whether we allow that love to pass through us to those around us is completely up to us. I'm convinced that Paul's grateful love for Jesus is what gave birth to the longing in his heart to visit the church in Rome and impart something to them that would benefit them individually and collectively. But Paul doesn't leave the statement in that posture of selflessness. He continues in the next verse by admitting what, I believe, is the best lesson learned from this passage: "That I might be encouraged together with you by the mutual faith both of you and me" (Romans 1:12).

The economy of the kingdom works in reverse. Jesus made this incredibly clear in His teachings, beginning with the Sermon on the Mount and continuing to His ascension into heaven. He made it astoundingly clear that we live when we choose to die (to self). We are esteemed when we take a posture of humility. And we get when we give.

Paul was calling this reversed approach to life to the forefront of the conversation and admitting that his longing for a visit to Rome was just as beneficial to him as it was to those he desired to bless.

Narrow Gate has allowed me to experience this truth in a way that few people are privileged to know. Countless friends and acquaintances have commented on how challenging it must be to live in constant community under the same roof with scores of students and interns on a 24/7 basis. But I can honestly say that the sense of purpose and fulfillment that my wife, Stacy, and I have gathered from this endeavor is far greater than any cost we've paid to see God's vision become reality for so many.

Paul knew this truth. I have been privileged to live out this truth, but far from perfectly or completely. It's worth considering how all of our lives would change if we saw dedicated sacrifice as the pathway to true richness in life.

Yes, Paul sought to bless the lives of the Roman believers, but he also understood that, in that process, he would be the one who truly benefitted. So, let's make the decision now to follow in Paul's footsteps, who was simply following in the footsteps of Jesus. Edify one another! Esteem one another! Encourage one another! And watch and see how God will edify, esteem, and encourage you.

> **Romans 1:13-14 |** "Now I do not want you to be unaware, brethren, that I often planned to come to you (but was hindered until now), that I might have some fruit among you also, just as among the other Gentiles. I am a debtor both to Greeks and to barbarians, both to wise and to unwise."

This introduction to the Roman epistle draws to a close with Paul repeating this idea of "getting in the giving." He openly admits that he wanted to have fruit among the Romans. But who benefitted from the fruit? Paul wanted the fruit that he might be the partaker who enjoys its existence. He stated that he was a debtor because he had been the one who reaped the fruit of the labor of Christ (who was his life).

If we do the work of planting and tending to the seeds of faith that God entrusts to us, won't we be the ones who get to enjoy the fruit of that labor? Too often, we consider how we are to count the "costs" of ministry without realizing that those costs might be better thought of as investments rather than expenses.

Finally, I feel compelled to make quick note of the fact that Paul included a spectrum of humanity here. Greeks were the cultured aristocracy of the world. They were the socially cultured elite who stood head and shoulders above the rest with regard to philosophy and art. But Paul indicated that he was indebted to the Greeks and barbarians, the wise and unwise. In other words, Paul had seen the effect of the gospel played out among the cultured, uncultured, wise, and not-so-wise.

Often, we fall into the practice of thinking that our ministry is to a specific group (culturally, socially, economically, racially, and so forth), but Paul dispelled that thinking by saying the gospel transcends socioeconomic boundaries. He credited the gospel as the power to transform life, and not his own ability to present it.

Once more, he was doing all he could to keep the light on Christ! The kingdom is, once more, presented as a reverse approach to the desired outcome: When I decrease, He increases. And as He increases, I am blessed in Him.

## Paul Announced He Is Ready to Preach the Gospel

**Romans 1:15-16 |** "So, as much as is in me, I am ready to preach the gospel to you who are in Rome also. For I am not ashamed of the gospel of Christ, for it is the power of God to salvation for everyone who believes, for the Jew first and also for the Greek."

Just for the record, this is the longest introduction to any of Paul's letters. I believe it's because he was writing to the only church that he wasn't able to establish and visit first-hand. So, after all of the language

that established his place in the body and his love for the Church, Paul was ready to preach the gospel in writing.

There are theologians who believe that the gospel presentation that Paul is about to present represents his earliest and most elementary beliefs regarding systematic theology. There are others who argue that this presentation is a much more sophisticated and mature approach to Christianity that came later in Paul's life. I don't think it actually makes a difference which stance a person takes. The syllogistic diatribe (posing an objection or problem and then answering that objection) makes a beautifully constructed presentation that fits our western minds perfectly. I think it might be beneficial to cover a couple of terms before we launch into the main body of Paul's letter.

First, the word "gospel" gets thrown around a lot in Christian discussion circles. Most people who are familiar with the term would quickly tell us that it means "good news", and they would be correct to some extent. But there's more to it than this simple definition would be able to supply. I like to use a true story to help the Narrow Gate Lodge students better understand the concept.

*Euangelion* is the Greek word that we translate "gospel" in the New Testament text. But if you look closely at the word, you might also see the origin of other words like "evangelism." The Christian faith has adopted and owned that word for the past couple millennia. However, the original form of the word had a different and deeper connotation that, while still true in the Christian sense, carried a very different conversational weight. But as I said earlier, I like to use a story to illustrate this weight.

In 500 BC, the Persians ruled the world. But no global rule is left unchecked, and in 499 BC the Ionian revolt began. The Greeks were

sympathetic to the Ionian resistance to Persian power, so they offered up support during the revolt. This show of support didn't sit well with the Persians who quelled the revolt in about six years. Once the revolt was put down, the Persians set out to teach the Greeks a lesson about opposing their rule.

In 490 BC, the Persians set sail for Greece with about 15,000 soldiers in tow. At this time, the Persian navy was far superior to the Greek navy, so the Greeks were able to offer little resistance to the oncoming Persian assault force. The first stop on the Persian invasion tour was the city of Eretria. The Persians easily defeated the Greeks at Eretria, and they followed the defeat with every imaginable torment to the citizens, including women and children, once the victory was in hand. But the next stop on the Persian tour toward Athens would be far different.

The Greeks knew that they needed to stop the Persians from reaching Athens or all would be lost. So, under the direction of their top general, Miltiades, they picked a battlefield that would give them every advantage. The Marathon Bay was that location.

The topography of the bay is marshy and narrow. That made it difficult for the Persian troops to maneuver because they were heavily armored and supported by a substantial cavalry. Yet the Greek army was outfitted very differently. They were primarily an infantry-based war machine. The Greek army was outnumbered 11,000 to 15,000, but it was a much more even match if the fight was constrained to an infantry event. Beyond the fact that Miltiades chose this advantageous battleground, the Greeks also presented a much more formidable infantry, which was populated by their foot soldiers called "hoplites." They carried lightweight shields and spears that could be lined up in ranks to form a phalanx.

The Persians landed their ships in Marathon Bay and lined up for battle. Miltiades intentionally weakened the center of his infantry defense to invite the Persians to try and penetrate the middle of the fighting forces. What the Persians did not know is that the hoplites could move much more quickly in the marsh than the Persians, and they were able to flank the Persian forces and cut them off from their reinforcements back at the ships. The battle that ensued was decisive, as Miltiades routed the Persian forces and brought a decisive victory to the Greeks, which proved to be a turning point in the Greco-Persian conflict. At the conclusion of the battle, Miltiades sent a runner named Pheidippides back to Athens to proclaim the outcome of the battle. And this is where our story becomes relevant to our discussion of the gospel.

The Athenians were all too aware of what the Persians had done to the women and children of Eretria. The horror of that aftermath was, in most Greek citizen's opinion, a fate worse than death. So, knowing the outcome of the battle of Marathon almost dictated the fate of the civilians left behind in Athens. If the battle in the marshy grounds of Marathon proved to be victorious, the citizens of Athens could rejoice because they had been spared a horrible fate. However, if the battle was lost, then the citizens remaining in Athens knew that torture, rape, and enslavement were just around the corner. They would be left with the choice to await their torture or to end their lives to avoid an inescapable outcome.

After twenty-five miles of exhaustion, Pheidippides burst into the chambers of the Acropolis with the proclamation: "Nike! Nike! Nenikekiam", which means "Victory, Victory, Rejoice, we conquered!" Those words served as the removal of a certain death sentence to the

citizens of Athens. There is a word for that sort of proclamation. It's called *euangelion*, which means "good news" or "gospel."

Gospel is not merely "good news." It is a declaration of victory in battle, announcing that the prospect of suffering and death has been alleviated for the people of a kingdom who were unable to prevent it themselves. Gospel is freedom from death row. Gospel is a last-minute pardon as you're guided down the hall to the gallows. Gospel is the absolute reversal of an absolutely certain negative outcome. It is rescue. Or, as Paul phrased it here: salvation.

The other word that we need to take a quick look at is *believe*. Paul said that the gospel is the power of God to salvation for everyone who believes, but if we're not careful, we can take that word a bit too lightly. He's going to follow this idea in the next verse with a quote from the Old Testament where he writes the word *faith*, rather than *believe*. If there is any interest in the original language that was used, these two words are *pisteuo* (believe) and *pistis* (faith). You can see that they share a common root, but one is an action verb and the other is a noun. This is where considering the entirety of Scripture becomes advantageous.

James later wrote some epistles where he qualified the fact that saving faith, or belief, is not an intellectual agreement to a stated fact. James 2:19 says, "You believe that there is one God. You do well. Even the demons believe—and shudder." He wrote these words while making the argument that recognizing Jesus as God is not the same as trusting Him to save you from the certain death that we just discussed. No demon has any trust that Jesus will stand before the Father as the defense attorney who has the paperwork necessary to rejoin their eternal existence back to their creator. As a matter of fact, I heard a discussion one time about the difference between factual confession

and saving confession. It goes something like this: If you were to ask the devil if God exists, he would quickly answer yes. If you were to ask him if Jesus was the Messiah sent to rescue humanity from eternal separation from God, he would answer yes. But Jesus isn't just "the" Messiah, He is "my" Messiah. Jesus' rescue was not only for humanity at large, it was for me personally. These are claims that Satan would never agree to.

Satan may recognize Jesus as the Messiah and Savior, but he could never see Jesus as his Messiah and Savior. The difference is an element of trust that is based in God's promise toward mankind as a whole, as well as you and me, individually. Moving beyond intellectual agreement and standing in active faith is what gives the gospel its power to save anyone who trusts in the intent and authority of its Author!

So, with this in mind, it seems logical to take a breath and consider how much of our "good work" is based in grateful response to the gift that has already been provided, and how much of that work is based in our attempt to garner God's approval to secure our place in His eternal kingdom. Thinking that our response to the gospel somehow earns or proves our standing with God actually diminishes our capacity for trust, and it also lessens the gratitude that we hold in our hearts for that screaming declaration, "Nike! Nike! Nenikekiam."

I don't want to oversimplify this concept too drastically, but I do want to finish this conversation with a story of a Narrow Gate student who asked a poignant question one night after a long Bible study. The question was a bit timid but monstrously genuine. He simply asked, "How can I know that I am saved?" Three questions came into my heart, so I just passed them along to him.

First: According to what you know of Scripture, do you believe that God wants people to be in His company or separated from Him? Now that's an easy one because Peter told us that "The Lord is not . . . willing that any should perish but that all should come to repentance" (2 Peter 3:9).

Second: According to what you know of Scripture, do you believe that God developed a mechanism for the fulfillment of His desire to have you back in His company? John 3:16 answers that one quickly.

Third: Are you depending on anything other than that mechanism (Jesus) to restore you into His company eternally?

It's really that simple. If we're depending on anything other than Jesus to restore the relationship between us and God the Father, we have false hope. Grasping this simple approach to salvation allows us to finally reach a point where we can say, "I may be a mess, but I'm His mess!" Thank You, Jesus, for saving me. Nike!

**Romans 1:17 |** "For in it the righteousness of God is revealed from faith to faith; as it is written, 'The just shall live by faith.'"

This verse contains an Old Testament quote that turned Martin Luther's life around and served as a treatise for the Protestant Reformation. In Latin, the doctrine can be labeled "sola fide" or "faith alone," and it declares that those who were once unrighteous or unjust will be declared righteous or justified through a single choice: faith.

"The just shall live by faith" is a quote from Habakkuk 2:4, and it serves as the driving thesis for this book, as well as Galatians and Hebrews. It was the shining hope of Martin Luther's life after suffering years of miserable self-assessment that left him convinced of his own

unworthiness in the sight of God. It was this verse and this concept that freed him from the tyrannical demand for righteous performance that was used by the Catholic church as a control mechanism over the uneducated masses of Europe in the dark times of history.

After discovering this verse, it became a cornerstone for Martin Luther's "justification through faith" systematic theology. He realized for the first time that his performance could never be good enough to win God's approval, so he stopped trying to gain the Father's acceptance through works and trusted Christ to bring him into a right relationship with God. From that point forward, Martin Luther sought to respond to God's grace with the posture, "I am saved!" This is the cornerstone of the gospel that Paul was about to preach.

To place a poetic exclamation point on the necessity of faith, Paul included the phrase, "from faith to faith" (Romans 1:17). He is subtly disqualifying ideas like faith to works; or from faith to knowledge; or from faith to piety. It is faith in Christ that offers salvation, and it is growing faith in Christ that continues to assure us during the life-long process of sanctification.

We'll close this section with a final thought: If you were in a court of law, each attorney would make an opening statement regarding the case about to be tried. If this letter to the Roman church was seen as the legal argument that it is constructed to be, we could now feel confident that the opening statement has been concluded. Paul spent the next seven chapters making and defending the argument that is built on the hypothesis, "The just shall live by faith!"

# Paul's Systematic Presentation of the Gospel

**Romans 1:18 |** "For the wrath of God is revealed from heaven against all ungodliness and unrighteousness of men, who suppress the truth in unrighteousness."

I always chuckle a bit when I read this passage, which seems odd, I know. There isn't anything funny about "the wrath of God." But I've tried to imagine what it would be like if someone asked me to make a gospel presentation, and I immediately launched into a diatribe about the wrath of God. I can't imagine that kind of conversation playing well in our modern society. But there are other ways to open the conversation with the same line of thinking but softer language. Let me explain what I'm writing about.

We could all agree that things aren't perfect in this world. Greed, pride, manipulation, and a thousand other forms of selfishness have woven their existence into society since the dawn of man's wandering outside the garden of Eden. That's why we've created laws and customs that are intended to control or correct the selfish choices that have the potential to do devastating amounts of damage to humanity. Society without regulation is no society at all. As a matter of fact, we do an exercise with the Narrow Gate Lodge students that asks them to define a list of words, one of which is "freedom." The majority of the students write something like, "The ability to do what I want to do when I want to do it." If you think through that answer, you'll realize that it is actually the furthest thing from freedom in a world where sin exists. Selfish choices that are allowed to be unchecked and unregulated become the pathway to anarchy.

Freedom, on the other hand, has a very different definition. After some discussion about the definition offered earlier, we offer up an alternative: "Freedom is the ability to move without constraint within a defined set of disciplines." And when those disciplines are overstepped or broken, we have social mechanisms to correct that behavior. It's dangerous to drive your car past a grade school doing 120 mph. So, to protect the children that depend on our love and care, we adopt laws that force drivers to slow their travel down to 20 mph. If you choose to disobey this law, the penalty is stiff.

To use an example that has a much broader and deeper effect, consider the stance that Teddy Roosevelt took against the corporate trusts of America in the early 1900s. Large and powerful companies figured out that they could form trusts that would allow all of those entities to be governed by a group of trustees. That gave them the ability to purchase goods at a deep discount and operate in a way that would crush any competitors trying to get a foothold in the marketplace. The result was a pricing model that was far more expensive than what the American public could afford, and the destruction of the American dream for many would-be entrepreneurs.

President Roosevelt used the Sherman Antitrust Act, formed in 1890, to take on the large, rich, and powerful trusts of corporate America and keep the dream of capitalistic opportunity alive for everyone. The fight was vicious, but in the end, the good of society prevailed against the greed of the aristocracy. Corrective measures had to be taken, or society would have suffered or maybe have even collapsed.

So, what does that have to do with this verse of Scripture? I think this verse begins to make clearer sense when we choose to pay attention to two specific ideas. The first is where God is directing His wrath.

We have a tendency to read the opening of this verse and think that God is directing His wrath toward a "who" instead of a "what." Yes, there are specific people listed in this verse—those who suppress the truth. But God's wrath is not being poured out on people. God's wrath is being revealed from heaven against the "ungodliness" and "unrighteousness" of those individuals, not the individuals themselves.

It might help to picture a surgeon in an operating room. I'm not sure how many of us have ever witnessed a surgery but some of them are brutal. An open-heart surgery has some violent and bloody aspects that could be seen as wrathful in their implementation. But if the surgeon doesn't take violent, corrective measures, the patient will die. So, whether it's removing a tumor or replacing a hip or fixing a malfunctioning heart, all of these procedures are, in the end, designed to save and improve life.

Just like Roosevelt taking on the corporate trusts of the early 20th century, or a surgeon taking on the violent and bloody process of life-saving surgery, God's willingness to expose man to His corrective choices are designed to help us live and thrive. Being able to fulfill whatever desire we have, regardless of the cost to those around us, is not freedom. It is enslavement to the selfish desires of a broken existence. God's corrective measures are not designed to destroy us; they are designed to set us on a path that leads to human flourishing.

I suppose a simple way to put what we're talking about is this: What we often see as destructive may be protective. God's wrath isn't aimed at humanity itself, but at ungodliness and unrighteousness—the real enemies, like a disease that leads to death. That leads us to a second thought about this verse that has real benefit—once we get our heads and hearts wrapped around the picture that it creates.

The ungodliness and unrighteousness in this verse is credited to people who have a specific habit. Paul said that those individuals "suppress" the truth, and the picture of Paul's statement comes to life when we understand the word *suppress*. The word is *katecho* (ka-tay-koh), and it was used as a nautical term to describe the process of a helmsman holding a ship against the direction that the water's current wanted to take it.

So, here we see Paul declaring that God's wrath is poured out against the ungodliness and unrighteousness that is manifested in people who know the truth, which is represented by the current. In Paul's linguistic metaphor, these people choose to steer their life in a direction that defies that truth. It's a practice that all of us have participated in at some point. We've known what was true or right in some circumstance but chosen to do what we wanted to do rather than doing what was right to do.

This leads me to believe, even more strongly, that God's wrathful expressions are directed toward the sin in this world that draws all of us off course and damages or destroys our lives. If someone you love was being influenced or attacked by an enemy that was determined to damage or destroy their lives, how aggressively would you defend that loved one? Keep that picture in mind as you read this verse.

Let's close this portion of the conversation with a quick question: Why would anyone know the truth of God's existence and yet fight against it? The answer is often as simple as this: If God exists, we are faced with a decision to remove ourselves from the throne of our lives and allow Him to be in control, or stay in "control" and do what we see as best or most desirable. Will God be God, or will we choose to suppress the truth and remain the god of our existence?

The choice is ours, but cost or benefit will always be close behind. Choose wisely.

I feel like we need to cover one more thing before we move on. In 1992, the world of cartoon animation was changed forever by the introduction of a new Batman series. The thing that made this animation different from all its predecessors was the choice of canvas that the artists used to create their stories. Until 1992, every animated series was produced almost entirely on white or clear backgrounds. But Bruce Timm and Eric Radomski chose to create the entire cartoon on a black background. The result was a finished work that allowed the color to pop dramatically against the dark and shadowy background. Paul chose to do the same thing in his presentation of the gospel. He painted a black and shadowy background of death and hopelessness so that the bright and bold colors of hope can leap from the story. Don't allow the dark and desperate language to throw you. Remember that the brightest dawn comes after the darkest night.

> **Romans 1:19-20 |** "Because what may be known of God is manifest in them, for God has shown it to them. For since the creation of the world His invisible attributes are clearly seen, being understood by the things that are made, even His eternal power and Godhead, so that they are without excuse."

One of the easiest ways to suppress the truth of God is to deny His existence. If we can rationalize that God is just a figment of our human social fabric, then we no longer feel compelled to subject ourselves to His sovereignty or dominion. Paul gave us these two verses to show us two different ways that God interrupts this futile and deadly attempt at independence.

Paul said that what may be known of God is manifested in everyone. Isn't it interesting that Paul immediately and subtly inserted the fact that man cannot fully know God by saying "what may be known of God" (v. 19)? This recognition stands in direct opposition to the idea that Satan presented to Adam when he said that disobedience to God would not result in death. Rather, it would result in man being on an equal plane with God by being "like God" (Genesis 3:5).

While man can never actually be like God, we can know certain things about Him by understanding the attributes of God that are manifested inside of us. This will be the first of two lines of thought that we'll cover as we discuss Paul's presentation in these two verses. The fact that things are manifested in us is the first thought, and the fact that things are clearly seen around us will be the second. These two thoughts have names and definitions in the world of Apologetics, which means a discussion in defense of something. So, let's look at those two arguments, but let's also remember that this short treatment of these verses is not designed to be a comprehensive treatment of the material. It's simply designed to begin a conversation between you and God, and if the Holy Spirit prompts you to dig deeper, you should fully respond to that prompting!

First, Paul called into play an idea that apologists would call the "moral argument." One of the more compelling aspects of the moral argument for God's existence is its appeal to the universal human experience of morality. Across cultures and societies, there is a common recognition that certain actions—such as kindness, honesty, or justice—are inherently good, while others—such as cruelty or injustice— are wrong. But we can be a lot more specific than that. It might be more effective to boil the argument down to this: If there is anything in this

world that is objectively right or objectively wrong, then that sense of morality must have come from something greater than people. However, if objective morality is not real, then nothing guides humankind through this journey of life except what we individually choose to think of as right or wrong.

We can put this idea to the test by asking the question: "Is it wrong to torture or kill innocent people?" Or "Is it right to defend innocent human life?" How do we answer questions like these if there is no universally acceptable standard for right and wrong? And who established that universal standard?

The moral argument proposes that this universally shared moral awareness points to the existence of a higher moral lawgiver: God. Rather than viewing morality as the subjective product of social evolution or personal preference, this perspective offers the idea that our moral intuitions are grounded in an objective source. To say it succinctly, if there is anything that is universally, objectively right or wrong then God must exist.

Paul took this stance in verse 19 by stating that God's nature of love and justice is manifest inside of humanity as evidence of His existence. But he didn't stop with that argument. He continued in verse 20 by moving the evidence for God's existence from internal to external. He moved from ethereal concepts like morality and conscience—which is just our highest known moral good—to more concrete concepts like the essence of nature and creation.

Paul's second set of arguments for the existence of God are typically referred to as the teleological and cosmological arguments. These two positions of defense center on the idea that if creation exists, there

must have been a creator. And, if design exists, there must be a designer. Let's take them one at a time.

It's challenging to deny that the echo of a "big bang" exists in the universe. The radiological name for this echo is the cosmic microwave background, or CMB. Feel free to dig into the specifics of this science if you choose, but it's compelling evidence that the big bang is real.

The scientific community refers to the existence of our universe prior to the big bang as the singularity. But the thing that is left unanswered is, "Where did the singularity come from?" It's fair to say that "something" doesn't come from "nothing." I know that this statement is a huge oversimplification, but it's a good place for us to begin the discussion with God as we move from question and confusion to balance and peace. If you're looking for a wonderful book that will help settle the conundrum between the days of creation listed in Genesis and the scientifically observable age of the universe, you might consider Gerald Schroeder's book, *Genesis and the Big Bang*. It is an amazing resource!

As a rational human being, I cannot align with the statement, "In the beginning, there was nothing, and then it exploded." However, if you want to take an agnostic or atheistic view of nature, then you are compelled to agree with that statement. When pressed, you may find that people who ascribe to this way of thinking will answer, "Given enough time, science will find a suitable explanation to make this statement true." But the thing I want us to realize is this: That statement is just as much a statement of faith as someone claiming that creation itself proves that there is a creator. In the end, there is no way to come to a final conclusion about the origin of the universe outside of faith. All of us line up evidence of varying sophistication and then come to a

conclusion based on that evidence. So, since we're aligning logic with evidence, let's introduce one more syllogism to the mix.

If there is design and purpose in nature, then there must be a designer. This is referred to as the teleological argument. We can understand it simply by using the illustration of someone walking on a beach. If any one of us were to take that stroll and find ornate and beautiful seashells, we could conclude that these are all natural products that belong on the beach. But if we found a pocket watch on the beach, we would never suspect that it naturally occurred. If there is a watch, there is a watchmaker. In the same way, no one would assume that a forest could give birth to an iPhone, or an ocean could create a cruise ship. It just doesn't make sense. Things with purpose and design precipitate the need for a designer.

So, if God's morality is woven into the fabric of our conscience, and the evidence of God's creation is woven into the creation in which we live, Paul argued that we are left without an excuse regarding the existence of our Creator. However, in the end, the choice to recognize God and give Him His rightful place in our lives is exactly that, our choice. We can either choose to follow the evidence for His existence and trust that He is who He claims to be, or we can place our faith in the intellect of mankind's philosophers and scientists and trust that, in time, we'll disprove God's existence and claim our rightful place on the throne of existence. And that is the exact dichotomy of thought that Paul dealt with next.

**Romans 1:21-23 |** "Because, although they knew God, they did not glorify Him as God, nor were thankful, but became futile in their thoughts, and their foolish hearts were

darkened. Professing to be wise, they became fools, and changed the glory of the incorruptible God into an image made like corruptible man—and birds and four-footed animals and creeping things."

There's a word in this passage that, if properly understood, can change our entire perspective on life outside of God's leading. The word is *futile,* but it's translated different ways depending on the Bible translation you choose to read. For instance, Ecclesiastes uses the Hebrew version of this word to open the entire book that Solomon is leaving behind for his son. But in that instance, it is most commonly translated *vanity* or *vain.* The King James Version uses that same word (*vain*) in Romans 1:21.

At its core, the word carries the connotation of something transitory. We might think of it as "pointlessness." I like to picture it this way when I'm trying to have a discussion with the Narrow Gate Lodge students. Do you remember planar geometry from your middle school days? The simplest element in planar geometry is the *point.* It's just a fixed position at the intersection of an X and Y axis that never moves. From there you can build line segments, rays, tangents, and so forth. But the "point" I'm making is this: If you don't have a point, nothing is fixed.

Imagine having a bouquet of helium balloons attached to a big rock. The rock becomes a fixed point. The balloons are free to move as much as they are capable of moving, depending on the strings that attach them to the rock. But if you remove the rock, the balloons wander wherever the wind takes them. They become transitory. The strings and the balloons stay attached and they are in the same relative relationship, but the thing that grounded them is gone.

Now translate that metaphor into real relationships where the untethered group is doing its best to make philosophical or spiritual decisions without a fixed point of ethical or moral good. It's like trying to navigate with a compass if there is no magnetic north. The outcome can never be something dependable or accurate because the basis for the decision—the grounding point—has been removed. That makes the collective decision futile, vain, or pointless.

That's the driving ethic behind Solomon's opening statement in the book of Ecclesiastes, where he says, "Vanity of Vanities. All is vanity" (1:2). This became the center of Paul's claim in Romans 1:21—that futile thoughts give way to darkened hearts. The result of that combined outcome becomes more well-defined as Paul continued his argument. So, let's move forward and look at how this decision to pointlessly deny the sovereignty of God plays out.

I think we've all encountered someone in person or in society who claims that adherence to Christianity is somehow parallel to foolish weakness in the hearts of the unenlightened masses who need a "god" to explain the things in life that they cannot control. They pronounce themselves to be the rationally enlightened leaders of humanity who have realized that science trumps faith. They have, therefore, conscribed issues of religion and faith to a lesser state of intellect. In other words, they have become *wise*.

To think that this is a new approach to life management is to be truly foolish. Since the earliest records, man has followed a pathway that is fairly predictable. We resist the idea that God should be sovereign because it takes authority away from us and places it in the hands of something other than ourselves. So, we seek to take back that control by becoming the supreme authority of our own existence. Isn't that the

exact argument that Satan made to Adam and Eve in the garden? "You will not surely die. . . . you will be like God" (Genesis 3:4–5).

Or, in some other cases, we choose to recognize that existence has a far greater reach than our perceivable reality. So, we turn to things that we marvel at like birds or powerful animals, or fascinating insects as an alternative to recognizing that there is a creator who made everything that "is" and then honoring that creator with the submission that is due. You may think that this is an outdated practice in our modern era, but if you travel to India and witness the cattle that roam the streets, you'll dispel that notion quickly. There are multiple examples of this ideology, but we get the point, right?

In the end, we'll find that people make horrible gods, as do birds, bulls, and beetles. When we exchange the glory of the incorruptible God for any earthly thing, we might as well dismiss the existence of deity altogether. And using scientific understanding as an excuse to ignore the existence of a creator is to place your faith in a construct that cannot provide comprehensive answers to the origins of existence. In the end, you will place faith into something; the question is *into what?* Paul was making the argument that worship is to be reserved for God alone. And while those who resist this current of truth may profess to be wise, simply saying something does not make it so. That is true foolishness.

**Romans 1:24–25** | "Therefore God also gave them up to uncleanness, in the lusts of their hearts, to dishonor their bodies among themselves, who exchanged the truth of God for the lie, and worshiped and served the creature rather than the Creator, who is blessed forever. Amen."

This is a pivot point of sorts for all people. It's as true a statement when applied to Adam and Eve as it is when it's applied to you and me. Thinking through the implication of this statement may help us see God in a way that is unexpected and astonishingly welcome. I know that, at first blush, this seems like a harsh statement of judgment on the part of God, and I'm not denying that it is exactly that. I'm not sure that's all that it is. Let me explain.

It's arguably true to say that the prevailing single-word description of God that is most encompassing and accurate is found in 1 John 4:8: "He who does not love does not know God, for God is love." Love. Not *loving* or *lovely* or *loveable*, although all of those things are true. God doesn't just love; He *is* love. There is no love that does not emanate from His existence. Since that is true, it means that there are conditions for how God relates to absolutely everything—including Himself. We don't have the time or space to fully explore all of the necessary conditions to prove that statement is true, but I don't think we can deal with this passage honestly if we don't consider one of those conditions.

The condition is: Love cannot exist outside of choice. That leads us to a syllogism that takes away the sting of judgment in this verse and begins to unfold a picture of mercy that will change our hearts, if we choose to let it. Here's the syllogism: God is love. We are made in God's image with a capacity for love. Love cannot exist outside of choice. Therefore, our relationship with God must have choice as a necessary component of the relationship.

When Paul wrote that man chose to exchange the glory of the incorruptible God for the corruptible image of man, birds, and so forth, that choice was the effect of God's willingness to enter into a loving relationship with us. It's easy to read this passage and have it play out in

our minds as God actively afflicting us for making poor choices. But the consequence of poor choice is not the active work of God. It's inherent in the nature of poor choices to have bad outcomes as a consequence. For instance, if I choose to jump off the roof of my house, gravity does not actively afflict me for making a foolish choice. If I choose to remove myself from God's will and nature in my life, God is not actively afflicting me for the outcome of my independent and sinful position.

I'm not stating that God does not create active, providential outcomes to curb the rampant spread of sin in this world. Instead, I'm saying that God will allow sin to have its negative effect—or even direct that negative effect—so that we can wake up and see the negative impact on our lives and turn back to Him in repentance.

To me the most amazing presence of mercy in this statement appears when you already know the fuller story of God's redemption through Jesus. Yes, God allowed Adam and Eve and all of us to make our independent, poor choices that led to our ultimate demise. However, knowing beforehand that we would make those foolish choices, God allowed us to experience our own destruction so that we could embrace His loving rescue with grateful hearts.

In a sense, it's like a parent allowing a child to make a poor choice that they know will have a difficult outcome, but knowing that they already have the solution in hand once the lesson is learned. Yes, God allowed us to pursue the selfish desires of our hearts, but He did so with the full awareness that rescue was in place for every single person who would reach the end of that selfish season and return to a Father who would welcome them with open arms.

What an amazing picture. I think of all the times that I haven't been allowed to "do what I wanted to do," and I consider the protective

hand of God. He simply will not allow me to do that which will cause irreparable harm. He allows me to wander, but He does it in a protective manner.

However, if left unchecked, this choice for independent control of our lives goes far beyond the idea of sexual immorality. That's just a mile marker on the highway of destruction that is paved with signs that things are bad and getting worse.

**Romans 1:26-28 |** "For this reason God gave them up to vile passions. For even their women exchanged the natural use for what is against nature. Likewise also the men, leaving the natural use of the woman, burned in their lust for one another, men with men committing what is shameful, and receiving in themselves the penalty of their error which was due. And even as they did not like to retain God in their knowledge, God gave them over to a debased mind, to do those things which are not fitting."

God is opposed to homosexuality. It is wrong (Leviticus 18:22). But so is fornication (Hebrews 13:4), adultery (Exodus 20:14), and lust (Matthew 5:28). They are all sexual sins, according to the Bible. But leaving it at that is far from sufficient for this quick discussion. The level of rejection that people feel when we spend our time telling them how wrong they are does little to express the love and mercy of God.

We live in a society and an era that declares that everyone should be allowed to love whomever they love, and in a certain way, I agree. Love is a gift from God. But how we love and how we live must be tethered to a moral compass that exists outside of our emotions, preferences,

or personal morals. We've already touched on this truth earlier in the chapter. So, yes, while I'm free to love anyone I choose, I'm not free to express that love in ways that step outside the will and nature of God.

I have dear friends who, by every human measure, are exclusively attracted to their same sex. And yet, they've never acted on those desires because they are bound by a higher love for Jesus. I also have friends who, if left unchecked, would be sexually active with every person of the opposite sex they could charm. And that posture is no less sinful than the homosexual mindset. These individuals choose to hold those desires in check because their love for God is greater than their desire for personal gratification.

The passage we're unpacking here specifically calls out the act of homosexual promiscuity as an example of how far the pursuit of selfish desires can carry us away from God's beautiful design for humanity. But it also rings the bell of vanity as Paul closed this section by making something clear: God will allow people who insist on autonomous rule to drift as far as they are willing to drift. That's the essence of a "de-based" mind. If there's no base—no anchor point of truth—then whatever makes sense to the independent mind of man becomes truth in that moment.

When this becomes the dominant voice in a society, the implications are devastating. There's a destabilizing effect that shows up every time everyone is allowed to do, say, or believe whatever seems right in their own eyes. This chaos doesn't stay in the margins; it moves into the very fabric of culture. History gives us a long line of civilizations that fell apart because they exchanged the pursuit of a common good for the hollow promise of personal autonomy. When personal autonomy becomes the highest social virtue, the resulting vacuum of

objective truth erodes the very structures that protect life, liberty, and flourishing communities.

Unchecked individual expression might feel like freedom at first, but eventually it leads to chaos where no one can agree on right or wrong, and the strong prey upon the weak. If you remove the common good, what's left is anarchy disguised as progress. It becomes every man for himself with no referee to blow the whistle and no higher authority to call a halt to the madness.

That's why God's boundaries—especially in areas like sexual ethics, covenant, and fidelity—aren't cruel constraints meant to crush our individuality. They're the loving guardrails that preserve both personal freedom and social stability. His ways aren't meant to kill culture; they're designed to hold it together. When we abandon those standards under the banner of progress or personal autonomy, we're laying the groundwork for the collapse of the very culture we think we're liberating.

God's boundaries protect both the individual and the community. His ways are always about life. The irony is that when we refuse to restrain our desires according to God's design, we think we're reaching for freedom, but in reality, we're reaching for chains. And we're dragging the whole culture down with us.

So, before we move on, if this verse has ever been used as a club to rail against the evils of homosexual freedom in our modern society, please let that stop here. Yes, wrong is still wrong. But Jesus reminded us that we'd better take a good hard look at our own independent postures before we take on the job of fixing someone else's life (Matthew 7:3-5). Paul reinforced that exact truth by including a list of behaviors that will show up anytime any of us choose to live outside the will and

nature of God. And by the way, that's every one of us at various times and in various ways.

> **Romans 1:29-32 |** "Being filled with all unrighteousness, sexual immorality, wickedness, covetousness, maliciousness; full of envy, murder, strife, deceit, evil-mindedness; they are whisperers, backbiters, haters of God, violent, proud, boasters, inventors of evil things, disobedient to parents, undiscerning, untrustworthy, unloving, unforgiving, unmerciful; who, knowing the righteous judgment of God, that those who practice such things are deserving of death, not only do the same but also approve of those who practice them."

Isn't it interesting—maybe even a little surprising—that Paul chose to pepper in things like *disobedience to parents* and *boasting* right in the middle of this scathing commentary on murder, sexual immorality, and hatred of God? It's one of those moments where we would do well to slow down and ask, "What do violence and wickedness have in common with something like a lack of mercy or discernment?" That kind of reflection can open the door to a much deeper understanding of how God interacts with us in our fallen state, and how easy it is for us to miss the point.

Maybe a good place to begin is with Paul's opening phrase in this section: "being filled with all unrighteousness" (v. 29). And yes, the word *all* means exactly what it says. All. I don't know about you, but I've held more than a few courtroom sessions in my own mind where I've gladly played the defense attorney and justified my behavior by comparing myself to someone I judged as more sinful. You know how

the argument sounds: "Well, at least I don't _____," and you get to fill in the blank. At least I don't murder. At least I don't act violently. But cuts through that flimsy defense with His words by reminding us that murder is just the extreme outcome of something much more common: anger, bitterness, and unforgiveness in the heart (Matthew 5:21–22). In other words, murdering someone's character through gossip or back-biting is just a different form of murder, but murder nonetheless.

Scripture is full of these types of insights. Ezekiel 16:49 is one that I like to remind the Narrow Gate students of. God Himself tells us what the sin of Sodom really was, and it's not the thing most of us immediately think of. God says, "Look, this was the iniquity of your sister Sodom: She and her daughter had pride, fullness of food, and abundance of idleness; neither did she strengthen the hand of the poor and needy." Only in the next verse does He get around to mentioning the more visible and extreme behaviors. In other words, Sodom didn't start with wild and destructive expressions of sexual avarice. It started with pride. With comfort. With laziness and self-satisfaction. It was an inside job, long before it ever became an outward catastrophe.

This ought to give all of us pause. It's easy to read this part of Paul's letter and think he was giving a laundry list of pagan atrocities, and to a degree, he was. But we'd be making a grave mistake if we didn't see our-selves somewhere on that same pathway. Maybe we haven't arrived at some of the more outward, culturally despised behaviors. But the first steps down the road are more familiar than we'd like to admit. Every time we choose to act according to our desires instead of God's design, we're taking that first step. We may not be sprinting toward rebellion, but we're on the road, nonetheless.

I think we need to ponder for a moment about how this doesn't just affect us individually. Paul painted a picture of what happens to an entire society when God is pushed out of the picture. When people decide that wisdom and self-reliance can replace the Creator, the ripple effects go far beyond personal sin. The breakdown of personal morality ripples into the breakdown of social trust, social order, and even the safety of the most vulnerable among us. When everyone does what is right in their own eyes, the center doesn't hold. Communities unravel, relationships disintegrate, and even the most basic institutions—like family, covenant, and truth itself—begin to collapse.

The balance between individual liberty and social stability has always been delicate, but it's only sustainable when it's tethered to something greater than ourselves. Left unchecked, personal freedom turns into social chaos. If we remove the fixed point of God's revealed standards—standards rooted in love, sacrifice, truth, and justice—then there is nothing left to guide the compass of culture. At that point, might makes right. Power dominates the powerless. The strong rule over the weak. And history shows us exactly where that leads.

That's why Paul's list feels so sweeping. It's not just about overt immorality; it's about what happens when human beings insist on playing God for themselves. The consequences spill out into every sphere of life. In the end, we see the terrifying spiral of not only doing what is wrong but celebrating it, approving it, institutionalizing it.

So, as we close this chapter, maybe it would be good for us to temper any enthusiasm we might feel about pointing fingers at the world around us. Every time you or I choose to act according to our desires rather than acting in accordance with the character and nature of God, we take the first step on that same journey of denial that Paul described.

To ignore God in favor of satisfying our personal wants is to take the seat of sovereignty away from Him and assume that position ourselves. I have yet to meet a person who hasn't done exactly that at least once, or maybe more honestly, dozens of times in their life.

Judgmental contempt is a dangerous posture to adopt. Paul dealt with that directly as he opens chapter 2. For now, maybe we'd all do well to sit quietly with these truths and ask the Spirit to show us where we've been tempted to exchange the glory of the incorruptible God for something much, much less.

# Review and Reflection— Romans 1

Let's slow down together and consider these questions as invitations to wrestle with the text in an honest, heart-level way. These are not just questions to answer; they're doorways into deeper conversations with God and with the people He's placed in your life.

1. **Identity Check:**

   When Paul introduced himself as both a "bondservant" and an "apostle," he was making a statement about *who* he was and *whose* he was. What's the significance of those two identities being held side by side? How does that challenge the way we see our own identity and purpose? Who does God say you are?

   _____

   _____

   _____

2. **Victory Proclaimed:**

   We talked about how the word *gospel* isn't just good news; it's a victory proclamation in the middle of a battlefield where death once seemed certain. How might that understanding reshape the way you see the message of Jesus in your own life? Is it possible that you've been living as if you're still waiting for a rescue that's already been declared?

_____

_____

_____

3. **Seeing God in All Things:**

   Paul made the argument that God has made Himself known both inside of us and in the world around us. Where do you see the fingerprints of God in creation, or maybe even more personally, in your own heart? Where do you struggle to see Him?

   _____

   _____

   _____

   _____

4. **Futile Thoughts and Darkened Hearts:**

   What comes to mind when you hear the word _futile_? How does the image of balloons without an anchor or a compass without north point stir something in you? Have you ever experienced a season where your thoughts felt untethered from truth? What happened? Where is your anchor point today?

   _____

   _____

   _____

5. **Human Autonomy and Its Consequences:**

   Paul wasn't just talking about personal sin; he was laying out a pathway of how entire societies drift into chaos when they try to rule themselves without reference to God's design. Where do you see that playing out in our world? Where do you feel the tension between your own desires and God's loving boundaries?

   _____

   _____

   _____

6. **From Personal Autonomy to Corporate Collapse:**

   This chapter makes a sobering observation: When the individual loses his or her compass, it eventually erodes the whole culture. How does that challenge the way you think about your personal choices, your family, your church, and your community? What would it look like to be an anchor point in the middle of that drift?

   _____

   _____

   _____

7. **Look in the Mirror First:**

   Paul's list of sins ends with a call to humility because if we're honest, every one of us finds ourselves on that list in one way or another. Where might you need to pause, lower your pointing finger, and invite the Spirit to search your own heart first?

   _____

_____

_____

## Heart-Level Reflections

These reflections are designed to linger in your spirit, not just in your head. I'd encourage you to take these reflective questions into your time alone with God, maybe journal about them, or even use them to open up a conversation with a trusted friend or mentor.

- **Am I Holding the Wheel?**

  Where am I gripping the wheel of my life, steering hard against the current of God's truth? What would it look like to release my grip and let God take me where He wants to go, even if that feels scary or unknown?

  _____

  _____

  _____

- **Love Requires a Choice:**

  We read about how love without choice isn't love at all. How does that truth help you see God's patience, His boundaries, and even His discipline in a new light? Where have you mistaken His protective "no" as rejection rather than love?

  _____

  _____

  _____

- **What Am I Trusting In?**

  If someone asked you, "What are you really counting on to make life work?", how would you answer? Is it really Jesus or is it your career, your comfort, your abilities, or your relationships?

  _____

  _____

  _____

- **Society's Drift and My Part in It.**

  When you look at the chaos of our culture, where is God asking you to stop wringing your hands and start becoming a voice of hope, truth, and love? What would that look like in your daily life, not just your theology?

  _____

  _____

  _____

# Prayer Prompts

Let's make these prayers a bit more like conversations. Imagine yourself sitting across the table from God, speaking from your heart and not reading off a script.

- **A Prayer of Surrender:**

  "Lord, I know I like to steer. I like to think I know best. But I confess, I've run my life off the rails more times than I can count. Would You remind me again today that Your ways lead to life?

I want to trust You with not just my eternity, but with the messy, everyday stuff of my life."

_____

_____

_____

- **A Prayer of Compassion and Humility:**

"Jesus, help me see the people I've been tempted to judge with Your eyes. Break my heart for them the way Your heart breaks for me. Let me speak truth, but always from a posture of humility, love, and grace."

_____

_____

_____

- **A Prayer for Courage in a Shifting Culture:**

"Father, it feels like the ground is shifting all around me. Help me stand firm in Your truth. Not arrogantly, but with the quiet confidence of someone who knows he is standing on the Rock. Show me how to be a light in a world that's lost its way."

_____

_____

_____

_____

# Action Steps

These aren't meant to be "To-Do" list items. They're invitations to take what we've talked about and walk it out practically this week.

1. **Take an Inventory:**

   This week, set aside thirty minutes to ask God, "Where am I resisting You? Where am I steering my life against Your current?" Write down what comes to mind. Don't overthink it— just listen.

   _____

   _____

   _____

2. **Reframe a Hard Conversation:**

   The next time you feel the urge to correct or challenge someone's lifestyle or belief, start by confessing your own need for grace first—maybe even out loud. See what happens to the conversation when you start from that place.

   _____

   _____

   _____

3. **Root Yourself in Truth:**

   Write out Romans 1:16-17 and post it where you'll see it every day this week. Let it remind you that the gospel is not just for the people "out there"—it's for you, right now.

   _____

_____

_____

_____

4. **Be the Anchor:**

In one relationship, one community, or one conversation this week, ask God to help you be the "fixed point" that offers stability and love in the middle of chaos. What might that look like? Maybe it's as simple as listening longer, speaking truth more gently, or showing up consistently.

_____

_____

_____

_____

5. **Pray Differently:**

Try spending one day this week practicing what we talked about: Keeping an open conversation going with God in the background of your heart, even while you work, drive, or talk with others. Notice how it shifts your posture.

_____

_____

_____

_____

CHAPTER 2

# Paul Addressed the Pretending Hypocrite

When we began our discussion of Paul's presentation of the gospel, we used the imagery of the 1990s Batman animated series. Paul painted the backdrop of human rebellion against God like a dark, colorless canvas. If God is light, and in Him there is no darkness (1 John 1:5), then when we attempt to remove Him from our lives, the only thing left is blackness—a suffocating, empty existence where mankind struggles to navigate a world without true direction or hope. This is the backdrop that Paul painted in chapter 1, as he exposed the desperate picture of life when we reject God as the rightful King.

Now, as chapter 2 begins, Paul pivoted to a new focus. He shifted from addressing the pagan heretic to addressing the pretending hypocrite. He had already demonstrated what happens when men try to dethrone God and crown themselves as their own moral authority. That rejection of God's rule leads to every imaginable kind of rebellion and self-serving behavior. Paul made it clear that ignoring God is not a passive act; it is the ultimate act of rebellion. Every other sin is just the inevitable fallout.

If that argument stands true, then the next logical step in Paul's case is unavoidable. If every person rejects God as the standard of truth,

then every person immediately sets up his or her own flawed and self-serving standards for right and wrong. When we do that, we naturally begin to compare ourselves to others—condemning others by our own arbitrary standards to make ourselves feel more righteous. Paul is about to show us that the very act of judging others by our own measure is the very thing that condemns us.

He wasn't talking about a sincere person struggling to live righteously while humbly acknowledging their failures. Paul was addressing those who use the moral failings of others as a stage to elevate their own self-righteousness, so they can avoid dealing honestly with their own sin. This is the heart of the issue as Paul turned the spotlight on the pretending hypocrite. Let's pick up the text and listen closely.

**Romans 2:1** | "Therefore you are inexcusable, O man, whoever you are who judge, for in whatever you judge another you condemn yourself; for you who judge practice the same things."

It's almost impossible to read this verse without immediately thinking of Jesus' famous warning in Matthew 7:1, "Judge not, that you be not judged." But it's crucial that we don't reduce this command into some simplistic, overused slogan that strips away its depth. This isn't a blanket command to never make judgments about anything. That would be absurd. Every one of us makes judgments every day of our lives—about people, choices, safety, right and wrong. It's part of what makes us human. So, what exactly was Paul saying here and how does it connect to Jesus' teaching?

It helps to know that the New Testament uses more than one word for *judge*. The word Paul used—and the one Jesus used in Matthew 7—is

the Greek word *krino*. The definition of *krino* is powerful. It means to distinguish, condemn, punish, avenge, or pass sentence with an attitude of contempt. It's an aggressive, hostile kind of judgment that declares another person condemned or worthless.

But there's another word for *judge* in the New Testament: *anakrino*. It's a softer word. It means to examine, to discern, to search carefully, to weigh evidence. This is the kind of judgment we admire in people with good discernment and wisdom. We see Paul use this form in 1 Corinthians 4, when he says he does not "judge" (*anakrino*) himself or others, because God is the one who sees all.

The contrast is clear: *Krino* is a judgment that leads to condemnation and contempt. *Anakrino* is a discerning examination that seeks truth and understanding. Paul was warning us about the first kind—the kind of judgment that pretends to have authority to condemn others while ignoring our own sinfulness.

Paul is about to advise us that this kind of condemning, contemptuous judgment is rooted in hypocrisy. The one who judges others harshly is often guilty of the very same things, whether in action, thought, or attitude. The one who points the finger at others does so to avoid facing his or her own sin. And that, Paul said, is the height of hypocrisy.

In chapter 1, Paul exposed the unrighteousness of those who reject God outright. But now, he was addressing the self-righteous who sit in judgment of others while blind to their own corruption. He moved from the pagan to the pretender. And it's not going to get any more comfortable as we continue.

**Romans 2:2 |** "But we know that the judgment of God is according to truth against those who practice such things."

Paul began his dismantling of the self-righteous position by reminding us that God's judgment is always according to truth. And that truth is not determined by human standards. God's truth will pierce through all the masks we wear and expose every hidden motive. Jesus made this clear when He said, "He who rejects Me, and does not receive My words, has that which judges him—the word that I have spoken will judge him in the last day" (John 12:48). God's standard is not arbitrary. It's the perfect truth embodied in Christ.

I can't help but think of Psalm 96:13b, where it reads, "He shall judge the world with righteousness, and the peoples with His truth." The standard is clear. Jesus, who never once violated the integrity of His identity, will judge all men. And He will judge hypocrisy most severely.

This is why we must pause to understand what hypocrisy is. The term comes from the theater of Paul's day. In Greek theater, actors wore masks and played roles other than themselves. The actors who played multiple roles were called *hypokrites*—hypocrites. They pretended to be something they were not. And that's exactly what Paul was addressing here. He was confronting the self-righteous person who pretends to be holy while inwardly corrupt.

Alexander the Great famously said he needed four elements to control the world: gymnasium, theater, schools, and church. It's the theater that best illustrates Paul's point here. Greek actors—always men—would play all the roles, donning different masks. Some actors were called *ithipoios* (character builders), but others—the *hypokrites*—took on all the rest, pretending to be whoever the scene required.

Paul was pointing out that self-righteousness is the ultimate form of religious hypocrisy—pretending to be righteous, pretending to be

good, while hiding our own sinfulness behind the mask of piety. This is the essence of what Paul dismantled.

So, in chapter 1, Paul exposed the unrighteousness of humankind. Now, in chapter 2, he exposed the self-righteousness of humankind. And as we'll see, both groups are equally in need of a Savior.

**Romans 2:3 |** "And do you think this, O man, you who judge those practicing such things, and doing the same, that you will escape the judgment of God?"

Let's not lose track of who Paul was talking to here. He wasn't narrowing his sights on the church. He wasn't looking at the pagan world exclusively either. He simply said, "O man." That's a big umbrella. He was talking to humanity at large—every one of us. It doesn't matter if you carry a Bible under your arm or a flask in your coat pocket. This is a word for anyone—especially those who think their religious face masks the rebellion still sitting in their heart.

This was Paul swinging the gate wide open and inviting everyone to consider whether their posture toward others is rooted in honest humility or arrogant self-righteousness. That's a hard question for anyone to answer with clean hands. Even the best of us is prone to playing the judge while ignoring the mess in our own house.

It's worth remembering that Paul was setting out to accomplish a goal. He was doing his dead-level best to position every human who has ever lived into the same predicament—the desperate need for a Savior. Whether our shortcomings are small and insignificant in our eyes or as obviously rebellious as the collection of characters described in the opening chapter, we are all in the same boat. Perfection is the standard, and we've all come up short. This is going to be the capitulation point of

his argument in just a few more verses. But, for now, Paul was just continuing down the path of holding up the mirror of perfection and asking every reader to do an honest assessment to see if the righteousness of his or her life will hold up to God's scrutiny in the day of judgment. I think we all know the answer to that one.

> **Romans 2:4** | "Or do you despise the riches of His goodness, forbearance, and longsuffering, not knowing that the goodness of God leads you to repentance?"

Paul moved the conversation to a place that ought to make us squirm a little. In essence, he said, "Are you despising the riches of God's goodness?" That's strong language. Most of us wouldn't use the word *despise* about God's kindness. But when you peel back the layers, we might be doing just that without realizing it.

Jon Courson gives us a helpful list of ways we can end up despising God's goodness.[2] Let's look at them quickly.

- **When others celebrate God's goodness in ways that make us uncomfortable.**
  Ever been in that spot? David danced before the ark of the covenant and his wife, Michal, rolled her eyes and despised him for it. She thought his joy was embarrassing. But what she really despised was a freedom she didn't have herself. Be careful when someone else's joy rubs you wrong. It might just be exposing something dry inside your own heart.

- **When God's goodness gets poured out on people we think are less deserving.**

That one stings. We see people who live in ways we don't approve of, and we want God to "deal with them." But when it comes to our sin? Oh, we want mercy and patience. Psalm 73 is a great case study here. The psalmist got frustrated that the wicked seemed to prosper while he was struggling. Jesus cut through this fog when He said the Father sends rain on both the just and the unjust. God's goodness doesn't consult our opinions before it gets poured out.

- **When we take advantage of God's patience to continue doing what we know is wrong.**

This one cuts deeply—at least it does for me. It's far too easy to think, *I'm getting away with it. God must not care that much.* Which is a cheap salve to soothe a guilty conscience. But inside we know that the justification is hollow and untrue. The truth is, He's giving us space to turn around before the consequences fall. Luke 13:6–9 shows us this. The fig tree wasn't producing, but instead of chopping it down, the vineyard keeper said, "Let's dig around it, let's give it more care." That's God's heart, but let's not mistake His patience for approval. The last line of that short parable reminds us that even the keeper of the vineyard recognized there comes a time when patient mercy has run its course and the truth must be faced and dealt with.

- **When we act as if repentance is optional or delay it indefinitely.**

Sometimes it's not defiance or entitlement that keeps us from repenting. Sometimes it's just drift. We don't mean to walk away. We just forget to come back. There doesn't appear to be anything catastrophic on the horizon, so we just keep heading that direction. Somewhere in the back of our minds we know

that we should turn around, but it just doesn't seem urgent. The warning here is that the longer we delay repentance, the more we risk hardening our hearts. The kindness of God is calling us—softly, gently, but also urgently. The longer we ignore it, the more likely we are to build a resistance we no longer feel.

The bottom line is God's kindness is meant to pull us toward Him, not to give us cover for staying in the mud. It's the undeserved, lavish goodness of God that should break us wide open and drive us to repentance. It's the contrast between what we deserve and what He offers that makes grace so powerful. And it's that very grace that gives us the courage to turn back to Him—not because we're scared of getting caught, but because we're overwhelmed by love.

**Romans 2:5-6 |** "But in accordance with your hardness and your impenitent heart you are treasuring up for yourself wrath in the day of wrath and revelation of the righteous judgment of God, who '*will render to each one according to his deeds*'" (emphasis added).

Paul shifted to a sobering image here. He said our hard, unrepentant hearts are actually storing up wrath like a man filling his barn with grain. But this isn't a harvest of blessing; it's a countdown to judgment. The imagery is intentional. The slow, steady accumulation of God's forbearance is not infinite. It's storing something. And if that space isn't filled with repentance and trust, it will be filled with something far more bitter. Make no mistake: There's a day on God's calendar, and on that day, there will be a full reckoning.

Don't miss the musical nuance tucked in Paul's language: "in accordance with" (v. 5). The phrase suggests harmony, like notes aligning perfectly in a chord. The wrath rendered will be in harmony with the hardness of the heart. God's judgment won't be an overreaction or a miscalculation. It will be in perfect alignment with what has been growing silently inside a person all along. The deeds don't just reveal the heart; they echo it.

This isn't God arbitrarily handing out punishments. This is God letting the end match the inward reality. Acts 8 tells us of s sorcerer named Simon. He did all the right religious motions, but Peter saw through it: "Your heart is not right in the sight of God" (v. 21). The outward posture was religious. The inward condition was self-centered and bitter. His deeds had the shape of faith, but the motive behind them betrayed him.

This raises a bigger point, one that threads through all of Romans: The deeds God will judge are not surface-level checklists. He's not grading moral behavior the way we grade homework. He's reading the motives behind the motions. That's why "doing good" isn't about religious activity; it's about a transformed heart bearing real fruit. Fruit that grows not by effort, but by connection to the root—Jesus.

Paul wasn't pitting works against grace here. He was contrasting the fruit of a softened, repentant heart with the hardened, self-justifying life. The result of each is rendered in kind. In other words, you will reap what you sow. Not just in behavior, but in belief, in motive, in the "secret" place.

Before we move on, I feel compelled to remind every believer reading these notes that "wrath" is reserved for those who have not turned their eternal outcome over to Jesus. If you trust Jesus to be your intercessor—like a defense attorney on the day of your life's trial—then

you've already bypassed God's wrath at the great white throne, which is talked about in Revelation 20. Instead, the events of your life will be tested by fire, according to 1 Corinthians 3, to see of what sort it is. Everything useless and sinful—which is anything done outside the will of design of God for your life—is likened to wood, hay, and stubble. Since it's tested by fire, it will simply burn away. But everything that is useful and beautiful in your life—which is anything done within the will and design of God for your life—is likened to gold, silver, and precious stones, which only get purified in the testing fires.

Don't read Romans 2:5-6 and get distressed because you believe that you're going to face the wrath of God almighty on the day of reckoning. Jesus already did that for you. He received the wrath that was set aside for your rebellion. The judgment that waits for you is more in line with our discussion of *krino* and *anakrino* in verse 1 of this chapter. Your life as a believer will be assessed for value and your heavenly reward will be handed out according to that assessment. It's the unbeliever who is claiming their self-righteousness as the measure of their worth who will face God's perfect standard in the day of judgment.

So, let's take note of how seriously God looks down on the act of self-righteousness and act accordingly. Let's avoid the temptation to begin feeling good about ourselves because God has allowed His grace to move us into a slightly more obedient posture than the people around us. Let's not lose sight of the fact that outside of grace, we are as lost as any other human being on earth. And then, let's allow the gratitude for this truth to compel us into a deeper state of humble submission to whatever Jesus would choose to do through us by the power of the Holy Spirit.

**Romans 2:7** | "Eternal life to those who by patient continuance in doing good seek for glory, honor, and immortality."

Here Paul held up a mirror to the life of someone who isn't living for applause or accolades but for something far more enduring. He's describing a person who is marked by *patient continuance*—that steady, faithful endurance that keeps showing up even when no one is watching. It's not a sprint. It's not a burst of effort. It's a life of consistent, God-centered perseverance.

And what are they seeking? Glory, honor, and immortality. Those three words are worth sitting with for a moment.

Glory is not about fame. It's about weightiness, substance. A life that has eternal meaning and reflects the character of God. It's that deep sense that our lives mattered—not just for now, but forever.

Honor is connected to identity. It's the confirmation that your life has been aligned with something righteous and noble. The world loves to dish out temporary honor—titles, trophies, blue checks. But Paul was talking about a lasting honor that only God can give.

And then there's immortality. That's not just about living forever; it's about living with God forever. It's about seeking a life that death can't erase. A life that's tied to a future beyond this world.

Paul wasn't saying that people can earn eternal life by doing good. That would contradict everything else he said in this letter. Instead, he's going to show what a saved life looks like. This is the kind of life that flows from a heart changed by God. This is the fruit of salvation, not the root of it. A person who's been transformed by grace begins to seek after different things. They start longing for God's approval more than man's approval. They aim their life at heaven, not just comfort.

This verse reminds us that the Christian life is more than a belief system. It's a trajectory. It's about direction, endurance, and hunger for things that are eternal.

> **Romans 2:8-9 |** "But to those who are self-seeking and do not obey the truth, but obey unrighteousness—indignation and wrath, tribulation and anguish, on every soul of man who does evil, of the Jew first and also of the Greek."

Paul gave us the other side of the equation. He wasn't being dramatic; he was being honest. There's a road that leads to eternal life, and there's a road that leads to anguish. The defining difference between the two roads isn't simply behavior. It's *obedience to truth* versus *obedience to unrighteousness.*

Let's take a closer look at that phrase: "self-seeking." The original Greek word Paul used was *eritheia*, which means "electioneering" or "canvassing for office." It describes someone who's obsessed with his or her own position, who works angles and manipulates outcomes to serve his or her own interests. In other words, the self-seeker is campaigning for the throne of his or her own life.

It's a haunting image because that's exactly what sin is. It's not just breaking a rule. It's running for a seat that already belongs to God. When we chase our own power, our own righteousness, our own control, we inevitably end up obeying unrighteousness. Not because we set out to be wicked, but because self-worship always leads there. You can't live for yourself and stay aligned with truth. One will eventually crowd out the other.

Paul warned us where that path leads: indignation, wrath, tribulation, and anguish. Each word steps deeper into the weight of judgment.

It's not just anger. It's a boiling over anger. A soul-deep tightness. A gnawing agony that begins here and stretches into eternity.

Again, Paul was careful to make this universal: "on every soul of man who does evil, of the Jew first and also of the Greek" (v. 9). No one gets a shortcut. No one gets a pass. Not the morally polished. Not the religious elite. Not the historically privileged. The law of sowing and reaping applies to all.

This is the leveling ground of the gospel. Every single one of us stands before God with the same problem and the same offer of redemption.

**Romans 2:10-11** | "But glory, honor, and peace to everyone who works what is good, to the Jew first and also to the Greek. For there is no partiality with God."

Paul brought the pendulum back to the promise that is held out for those who live a life aligned with God's heart—glory, honor, and peace. This peace isn't just the absence of trouble. It's the Hebrew idea of *shalom*—wholeness, flourishing, rest. A peace that goes deeper than circumstances and stretches into eternity.

Paul wasn't presenting a works-based salvation. He was pointing to a works-reflecting salvation. There's a kind of life that shows who we belong to. And that life is marked not by self-seeking, but by God-seeking. Not by grasping, but by surrender. Not by manipulation, but by faithfulness.

Paul tied it all together with this profound declaration: "There is no partiality with God" (v. 11). In the ancient world, partiality was assumed. Kings had favorites. Priests had special access. The religious system often catered to those with power or pedigree. But Paul said that this

isn't the case with God. His justice isn't swayed by titles, birthrights, or resumes. His grace isn't earned by status or lineage. God sees through the categories we've built and cuts straight to the heart.

This is both beautiful and terrifying. It means the proud have no advantage, and it means the humble have full access. It means your past doesn't disqualify you, but your pride might. It means that God doesn't grade on a curve. He offers mercy to all and demands honesty from all.

When Paul said there is no partiality with God, he wasn't just stating a fact. He's swinging the door wide open for anyone willing to walk through it in humility. Jew or Gentile. Scholar or shepherd. Outcast or insider. The ground at the foot of the cross is beautifully level.

**Romans 2:12 |** "(for as many as have sinned without law will also perish without law, and as many as have sinned in the law will be judged by the law."

Paul aimed directly at a mindset that would have been deeply ingrained in his Jewish listeners—the belief that possession of the Law itself made them special or safe. Paul's logic slices right through that illusion: *It's not about whether you have the Law, it's about whether you've obeyed it.*

Let's unpack the two groups Paul named in this verse. First, there were those who sinned without the Law. That's the Gentiles. They didn't grow up with Torah scrolls in their homes. They weren't raised quoting Moses or rehearsing the feasts. But Paul said their ignorance didn't make them innocent. They would still perish. Not because they didn't have the Law, but because they still sinned.

Then Paul turned to those who had sinned under the Law: the Jews. These were the people who knew the Law, revered the Law, and

memorized the Law. And yet, knowledge didn't keep them from falling short. If anything, it made them more accountable. Their judgment would be based on the very truth they knew.

It's easy to see how this logic applies far beyond Paul's original audience. We could say the same thing today: Those who have never set foot in a church will be judged differently than those who have spent their lives in pews. But in both cases, sin still separates. Knowing better doesn't equal living better, and not knowing doesn't equal being better.

Paul wasn't leveling the playing field to shame anyone. He was doing it to expose the only real hope anyone has. Not knowledge, not heritage, not effort. Just grace. He was carefully dismantling the prideful idea that some people are "less lost" than others.

> **Romans 2:13 |** "For not the hearers of the law are just in the sight of God, but the doers of the law will be justified."

This is where Paul tightens the net. He was building toward this moment. You can almost hear the collective "amen" from the Jewish readers after verse 12: "Yes! The Gentiles without the Law are clearly guilty!" But Paul didn't let that self-congratulatory tone hang in the air for long. Here's the twist: Just hearing the Law doesn't make you righteous. Obedience to the Law is what matters.

That would have landed like a punch to the gut. The Jews prided themselves on hearing the Law read aloud in the synagogue, on memorizing long passages of Scripture, on parsing every command and nuance. But Paul was saying that none of that matters unless it actually changes how you live.

It's like a person who owns every classic cookbook but never cooks a meal. Or a guy who goes to the gym six days a week, listens to health

podcasts, and wears all the gear but never breaks a sweat. Paul's exposing the gap between *knowing* and *doing*.

And just to be clear, Paul wasn't suggesting that salvation comes from doing the Law perfectly. He will soon make the case that nobody can. He was simply showing that knowledge alone doesn't save. God doesn't hand out righteousness for sitting through lectures or reciting facts. He's after transformation, not information.

> **Romans 2:14-15 |** "For when Gentiles, who do not have the law, by nature do the things in the law, these, although not having the law, are a law to themselves, who show the work of the law written in their hearts, their conscience also bearing witness, and between themselves their thoughts accusing or else excusing them)."

Paul goes back to the Gentiles to finish building his argument. Even though they didn't have the Law written on scrolls or spoken by rabbis, they had it written on their hearts. That's the power of conscience.

Think about that for a moment. From the earliest days of human history—long before laws were written in stone—people had an internal sense of right and wrong. They knew it was wrong to steal, wrong to kill, wrong to betray. Why? Because the God who made them also stamped a moral code into their DNA. It's why even young children, without ever reading a moral philosophy book, will cry, "That's not fair!" Something inside all of us bears witness to the moral order of the universe.

Paul said that the Gentiles demonstrated this in real time. Their thoughts either accused or excused them. That's conscience at work. It's the internal courtroom every person carries around—the one that tries to justify or condemn our behavior, even when no one else sees.

Now, conscience isn't infallible. It can be shaped, dulled, even corrupted. But it's still evidence that humanity is wired with a sense of accountability. This is Paul's point: Whether you have the written Law or not, God has placed enough truth in your heart to make you morally responsible.

So, when the Gentile acts in a way that aligns with God's law (say, by caring for the poor, honoring parents, or showing mercy), they're not earning salvation. They're proving that the law is already echoing inside them, even without a scroll or a sermon.

This raises a crucial point: Everyone knows more than they obey. Which means no one—Jew or Gentile—has room to boast.

**Romans 2:16 |** "In the day when God will judge the secrets of men by Jesus Christ, according to my gospel."

Paul landed this portion of his argument with a clear and chilling truth: There is a day coming when God will judge not just actions but secrets, and He will do it through Jesus Christ.

This is where all of Paul's logic has been pointing. Not toward a list of dos and don'ts, but toward a Person. Jesus is the standard. Not Moses. Not tradition. Not your neighbor. The one who will judge the world is the very One who laid down His life for it.

And this judgment will reach into the secret places. The hidden motives. The behind-the-scenes decisions. The attitudes we excuse and the thoughts we never say out loud. God isn't limited to evaluating our performance. He sees what no one else sees.

That could be terrifying if not for the last phrase: "according to my gospel." Paul wasn't just talking about judgment; he was pointing to the gospel as the only safe refuge. The One who will judge the world is also

the One who took the world's judgment upon Himself. The gospel says that Jesus absorbed the penalty you deserved so that on that day, when every secret is laid bare, your story can still end in mercy.

That's why Paul's gospel isn't just good advice. It's good news; it means you don't have to hide anymore. You can bring your secrets into the light and find that grace has already made a way.

> **Romans 2:17–20 |** "Indeed you are called a Jew, and rest on the law, and make your boast in God, and know His will, and approve the things that are excellent, being instructed out of the law, and are confident that you yourself are a guide to the blind, a light to those who are in darkness, an instructor of the foolish, a teacher of babes, having the form of knowledge and truth in the law."

Paul turned his gaze directly toward his Jewish brothers, and he affirmed what they would have proudly accepted as their identity. You rest on the Law. You boast in your relationship with God. You know His will. You've been shaped and instructed by the Scriptures. You believe you're a guide, a light, a teacher. Someone who helps others find their way.

And honestly, none of those things are inherently wrong. In fact, they represent a tremendous spiritual privilege. God revealed Himself to Israel in ways the surrounding nations could only imagine. He gave them His commandments, His covenants, His presence. They were meant to be a light to the nations. Not just a holy club, but a living demonstration of what it looks like when a people walk with God.

But here's the problem Paul is about to expose: Privilege without humility breeds arrogance. And spiritual advantage without inward transformation becomes the perfect breeding ground for hypocrisy.

There's a subtle warning here for those of us who've grown up in church culture. It's possible to be surrounded by truth—to hear sermons, memorize Scripture, serve in ministry—and still miss the very heart of God. We can become so confident in our role as guides that we forget we're also travelers. So confident in our status as instructors that we stop being students ourselves. The danger is not in knowing much. It's in thinking that our knowledge alone makes us right with God.

> **Romans 2:21-24 |** "You, therefore, who teach another, do you not teach yourself? You who preach that a man should not steal, do you steal? You who say, 'Do not commit adultery,' do you commit adultery? You who abhor idols, do you rob temples? You who make your boast in the law, do you dishonor God through breaking the law? For 'the name of God is blasphemed among the Gentiles because of you,' as it is written."

Here comes the pivot. Paul turned all those affirmations into a mirror, and the reflection isn't flattering.

He was essentially saying: If you're the teacher, have you learned the lesson yourself? If you're the one preaching about theft, are you stealing in some hidden way—financially, relationally, emotionally? If you stand against adultery, is your heart pure in thought and action? If you denounce idolatry, are there still altars in your life disguised as ambition, approval, or pride?

It's easy to read this as a finger-pointing rant, but that would miss the heart of Paul's concern. This isn't condemnation for its own sake. It's an invitation to self-examination.

And the stakes are high. Paul didn't just say, "You've missed the mark." He was saying, "Your hypocrisy has damaged the witness of God Himself." The name of God is being blasphemed among the Gentiles— not because of paganism, but because of religious inconsistency. That's a sobering indictment.

The people who were meant to represent God to the world had, by their hypocrisy, become a reason for the world to mock Him. Instead of being a light to the nations, they'd become a warning label.

And again, we must be honest enough to see ourselves here too. How many people today reject Christianity not because of Christ, but because of how Christians behave? How many times have we seen spiritual leaders fall, or churches become known more for division than compassion?

It doesn't mean we have to be perfect, but it does mean we must be authentic. The world can handle imperfection. What it struggles to handle is inconsistency that pretends to be holy. What Paul was calling for isn't performance; it's integrity. A life where what we teach others is first being lived in us.

> **Romans 2:25 |** "For circumcision is indeed profitable if you keep the law; but if you are a breaker of the law, your circumcision has become uncircumcision."

Paul tackled one of the most sacred symbols of Jewish identity— circumcision. For the Jewish people, circumcision wasn't just a tradition. It was a covenantal sign. It marked their connection to Abraham, their inclusion in the promises of God, their distinction from the surrounding nations. To be circumcised was to belong.

Paul challenged that assumption head-on. He said, in essence: *Yes, circumcision has value, but only if it reflects a life of actual obedience.* If you break the law, the sign you wear on your body doesn't matter. The mark becomes meaningless. The badge of belonging carries no weight if the life underneath it is disconnected from the God it claims to honor.

This would've been incredibly difficult for many Jews to hear. They had been raised to see circumcision as the non-negotiable proof of covenant. But Paul peeled back the layers to reveal something deeper. Outward rituals can never substitute for inward reality. The sign is only as significant as the sincerity behind it.

We're not immune to this trap today. We may not boast in circumcision, but we often lean on our own badges—church attendance, baptism, Bible knowledge, family heritage, moral behavior. And while those things can all be good, none of them justify us before God. They're not the foundation of our identity. They're meant to be expressions of something deeper.

Paul's point was simple but piercing: External religion is powerless to save if the heart remains unchanged.

> **Romans 2:26-27 |** "Therefore, if an uncircumcised man keeps the righteous requirements of the law, will not his uncircumcision be counted as circumcision? And will not the physically uncircumcised, if he fulfills the law, judge you who, even with your written code and circumcision, are a transgressor of the law?"

Here Paul flipped the equation. If a Gentile—someone uncircumcised, someone outside the formal covenant—lived in alignment with

the heart of God's law, wouldn't his or her obedience mean more than the ritual he or she lacks?

To Paul's audience, this was revolutionary. He was saying that faithfulness matters more than form. That obedience from the heart counts more than symbols on the body. That someone from the "outside" who walks with God can, in a very real sense, be more aligned with the covenant than someone from the "inside" who violates it.

Then Paul dropped a provocative image: That Gentile, the one you may have looked down on, might actually stand in judgment over you. That would have been unthinkable for many Jews of Paul's day. But it's the logical outcome of Paul's argument. If covenant is truly about relationship with God, then those who walk with Him—even without the outward symbols—have more credibility than those who bear the marks but not the heart.

This challenges all of us to ask a hard question: Are we more concerned with the appearance of spirituality than the substance of it? Are we clinging to religious identity without allowing God to shape our actual character?

It's not enough to be born into the right family, attend the right church, or say the right things. Paul was dismantling any version of faith that depends on heritage or external markers. What God wants isn't compliance. It's transformation.

> **Romans 2:28-29 |** "For he is not a Jew who is one outwardly, nor is circumcision that which is outward in the flesh; but he is a Jew who is one inwardly; and circumcision is that of the heart, in the Spirit, not in the letter; whose praise is not from men but from God."

This final verse brings the entire argument to its crescendo. Paul redefined identity—not based on external appearance, but on internal reality. Not based on heritage, but on heart. He said that true covenant people are those who have experienced a circumcision of the heart, a spiritual transformation that cuts away the old nature and replaces it with new life in God.

This wasn't a new idea, either. The prophets had spoken of this long before Paul. Deuteronomy 30:6 says, "The LORD your God will circumcise your hearts . . . [so that you may love Him] with all your heart and with all your soul, and that you may live" (emphasis added). Jeremiah spoke of uncircumcised hearts as a way of describing people who were physically marked as God's people but internally resistant to Him (Jeremiah 9:25-26).

Paul now carried that theme into full clarity. The mark God is looking for is not on the skin; it's on the soul. And that work can't be done by man. It must be done by the Holy Spirit.

He ends with a powerful phrase: "whose praise is not from men but from God" (Romans 2:29). That's what we're after, isn't it? Not applause, not approval from religious communities, not affirmation from peers, but that quiet, soul-settling affirmation that comes from the Father: "Well done."

This chapter ends not with condemnation, but with invitation. Lay down your masks. Let go of the empty badges. Stop managing appearances. Let the Holy Spirit do the deep work of transformation in your heart. That's where true covenant begins. And that's where the gospel comes to life.

# Review and Reflection— Romans 2

**L**et's sit with these questions for a while. Don't rush past them like a quiz; let them open the door to some honest conversations between you and God. Maybe even use these questions to stir up dialogue with people you trust to tell you the truth in love.

1. **The Pretender in the Mirror:**

   Paul shifted his focus in chapter 2 from the obvious rebel to the pretending hypocrite—the one who hides behind morality, religion, or good behavior to avoid facing their own sin. Where do you see that tendency in your own life? Are there areas where you project righteousness on the outside but resist letting God deal with what's going on inside?

   _____

   _____

   _____

2. **Judging or Discerning:**

   We talked about the difference between *krino* judgment (condemning, contempt-filled) and *anakrino* judgment (discerning, examining carefully). Which one comes more naturally to you?

How can you grow in practicing godly discernment while avoiding the trap of self-righteous condemnation?

_____

_____

_____

3. **Despising God's Kindness:**

Paul said we can actually "despise" God's kindness when we misuse it as a cover for our sin or grow numb to His mercy. Where in your life have you mistaken God's patience as permission? How does His kindness invite you to repentance—not out of fear but out of gratitude?

_____

_____

_____

4. **Self-Righteousness on Display:**

When you read the list of ways people boast in their own goodness while still falling short (preaching "don't steal" while stealing, and so forth), where do you feel the Holy Spirit tapping on your heart? Are there ways your life has projected one thing while hiding another? What would it look like to bring that into the light—maybe for the first time?

_____

_____

_____

## 5. The Hidden Places:

Paul made it clear that God isn't just looking at our behavior; He's judging the secrets of our hearts. What are some of the "secret places" in your heart where you've avoided letting God speak? What would it take to invite Him into those places?

_____

_____

_____

## 6. No More Masks:

Paul painted a picture of faith that's not about outward signs or rituals, but about an inward, Spirit-led transformation. Where are you tempted to rely on your religious habits or identity instead of a real, ongoing relationship with Jesus? What might it look like this week to take off the mask and walk in honest surrender?

_____

_____

_____

## 7. One Family Under Christ:

Paul reminded us that there are no more dividing walls in Christ—no Jew, no Gentile, no "better group." How might you still be holding on to categories that Jesus tore down? Where do you see pride or partiality creeping into your thinking about yourself or others?

_____

_____

_____

## Heart-Level Reflections

I encourage you to let these reflections soak into your spirit over the next few days. Maybe even write them in your journal and see where God wants to meet you in them.

- **Am I Playing the Part?**

  Have I become more comfortable playing the role of the "good Christian" than actually walking in humble dependence on Jesus? What's one area where I can stop performing and start being real?

  _____

  _____

  _____

- **Goodness That Leads to Change:**

  How does it change the way I see God when I remember that His kindness—not His anger—is what leads me to change? Where have I resisted that kindness because I was afraid of what it might require of me?

  _____

  _____

  _____

- **Do I Really Want God to Be God?**

  If I'm honest, are there places where I still want to be the one in control? Places where I resist God's right to call the shots? What would it look like to let Him back on the throne of those areas?

  _____

  _____

  _____

# Prayer Prompts

Use these prompts as the start of a conversation. Let them breathe. Let them get under your skin.

- **A Prayer for God to Search My Heart:**

  "Father, it's easy for me to see the sin in others. It's harder to let You show me what's still hiding in my own heart. Would You search me today? Expose the places where I'm still playing games with You. And when You do, give me the courage to run toward You and not away from You."

  _____

  _____

  _____

- **A Prayer of Gratitude for His Kindness:**

  "Jesus, thank You that You are so patient with me. Thank You that You haven't given me what I deserve, but instead You keep pouring out grace and kindness to lead me home. I don't want to take that for granted. Help me respond with an open heart and willing hands."

_____

_____

_____

- **A Prayer to Remove the Mask:**

  "Spirit of God, tear off the masks I've been wearing to impress others or to hide from You. I want to live in the freedom of being known and loved by You. Not performing, not pretending, but trusting that You see me, You know me, and You still call me Yours."

  _____

  _____

  _____

## Action Steps

These steps aren't about performance; they're invitations into a deeper, freer, more authentic walk with Jesus this week.

1. **Name the Mask:**

   Spend some time this week asking God to show you any place in your life where you're pretending. When He shows you, write it down. Name it. Confess it. Don't hide from it.

   _____

_____

_____

2. **Extend the Kindness You've Received:**

   Paul reminded us that it's the goodness of God that leads to change. This week, look for one person in your life who needs to see that same goodness from you. Instead of judgment, what would it look like to extend compassion and mercy?

   _____

   _____

   _____

   _____

3. **Quiet the Boast:**

   If you catch yourself boasting—whether out loud or in your head—pause. Ask God to remind you that your only boast is Jesus. Practice humility by intentionally giving thanks for His work in your life, rather than trying to prove yourself.

   _____

   _____

   _____

   _____

4. **Look at the Secret Places:**

   Find a quiet space and ask the Holy Spirit to shine His light on the "secret places" Paul talked about. What's hiding in the corners of your heart? When He shows you, invite Him to meet you there with His grace.

_____

_____

_____

_____

5.  **Choose Heart Over Habit:**

    This week, take one of your spiritual habits (Bible reading, prayer, church attendance, and so forth) and pause before doing it. Ask yourself, "Am I doing this as an outward ritual or as an act of love and surrender to Jesus?" Let that awareness reshape the way you engage with Him.

    _____

    _____

    _____

    _____

CHAPTER 3

# God's Righteousness Is the Standard for Judgement

**Romans 3:1-2 |** "What advantage then has the Jew, or what is the profit of circumcision? Much in every way! Chiefly because to them were committed the oracles of God."

Paul anticipated the pushback. If everyone—Jew and Gentile alike—was under sin and in need of grace, then what was the point of all that came before? Why did God set apart a people, give them the Law, mark them with circumcision, and call them His own? Was it all meaningless?

Not at all. Paul responded emphatically: There is advantage—great advantage—in being part of the Jewish covenant community. Why? Because they were entrusted with the very oracles of God. Not just moral rules or cultural traditions, but the actual words of the Living God—spoken, preserved, cherished, and handed down through generations. All of it—the Torah, the prophets, the psalms—formed the sacred trust God placed in the hands of His people. It's those very oracles that

have allowed the Jewish people to thrive for centuries since the establishment of the covenant.

It's critical to see what Paul didn't say. He wasn't claiming that the Jews had a moral edge or a salvation shortcut. The advantage wasn't in immunity from judgment, but in intimacy with revelation. The oracles of God didn't make them more righteous; they made them more responsible.

Imagine holding a map in your hands while the rest of the world walks in darkness. That's what it meant to be entrusted with God's Word. It's a privilege, but it's also a burden, because you're not just accountable for your choices; you're accountable for what you've been shown.

This sets the stage for Paul's next point. Revelation is a gift, but it doesn't exempt us from the need for redemption.

**Romans 3:3-4 |** "For what if some did not believe? Will their unbelief make the faithfulness of God without effect? Certainly not! Indeed, let God be true but every man a liar. As it is written: 'That You may be justified in Your words, and may overcome when You are judged.'"

Paul shifted his writing to address another subtle question. If the Jewish people failed to believe, did that failure somehow derail God's plan? Did their unbelief nullify His faithfulness? It's the type of questions that creeps into all of our hearts at some point: Can human failure cancel divine purpose? Can my "badness" cancel out God's "goodness" and His plan to save me?

Paul's answer couldn't be clearer: Absolutely not. "Let God be true, though every man a liar" (v. 4). In other words, God's character does

not hang on the thread of human cooperation. He is faithful—*period*. Even when we're not.

Paul used a quote from Psalm 51, where David—broken over his sin—confessed that God was justified in His judgments and blameless in His words. David acknowledged something in which Paul applied on a much larger scale: God is always right. Even when His people are wrong.

This truth is both humbling and comforting. It humbles us because we can't leverage God's promises against Him, as if our disobedience makes Him the villain. And it comforts us because God's covenant faithfulness is never dependent on flawless people. He keeps His promises even when we falter. He carries His plan forward even when we lag behind.

In other words, our inconsistency never compromises His integrity.

**Romans 3:5-6 |** "But if our unrighteousness demonstrates the righteousness of God, what shall we say? Is God unjust who inflicts wrath? (I speak as a man.) Certainly not! For then how will God judge the world?"

In these verses, Paul engaged in a type of hypothetical debate. It's a line of reasoning that probably came from his critics, and maybe even surfaced within the early church: *If our sin somehow serves to highlight God's righteousness, doesn't that make our sin useful? Isn't God unfair to judge us for something that ultimately makes Him look good?*

Paul cut through this twisted logic immediately. "Certainly not!" (v. 6). That's his way of slamming the brakes on a reckless argument. If God were unjust to inflict wrath, then He'd have no grounds to judge anyone. And yet, the judgment of the world is a foundational truth. It's

written into the conscience of man and the pages of Scripture. Without divine judgment, there's no moral order. No accountability. No justice. Everything unravels.

Paul reminds us: God is not running a PR campaign. He's not in the business of using our sin to boost His image. God is holy. He's just. And when God judges sin, it is not a contradiction of His goodness; it is an expression of it.

If we ever start thinking that our sin somehow benefits God, we've slipped into absurdity. Sin isn't a tool that helps God out. It's a sickness that required the blood of His Son to heal us. That should settle the matter.

> **Romans 3:7-8 |** "For if the truth of God has increased through my lie to His glory, why am I also still judged as a sinner? And why not say, 'Let us do evil that good may come'?—as we are slanderously reported and as some affirm that we say. Their condemnation is just."

Paul pushed the faulty logic to its final, grotesque conclusion. If our sin makes God look better, why not sin more? If grace shines against the backdrop of our rebellion, shouldn't we just keep painting with darker strokes, so His goodness pops even more?

This, Paul said, is where distorted theology ends up—in license, in blasphemy, and in condemnation.

Apparently, some were falsely accusing Paul of preaching this very idea—that his gospel of grace gave people a free pass to live however they pleased. Paul didn't waste time defending himself. He simply said that those who teach such things will face the judgment they deserve.

This is a good reminder that even the purest gospel can be twisted. Grace has always been scandalous. The idea that God justifies the ungodly—that He declares the guilty righteous because of Christ—has always offended human pride. So, it's no surprise that some would take that offense and turn it into slander. Paul wasn't rattled by it, but he was clear: Grace is never an excuse for sin. It is the reason we flee from it.

Imagine a man drowning in the ocean, lifted out by a rescuer, revived on the shore, and then saying, "That was incredible. Let's do it again!" It would be madness. When we've truly experienced rescue, the last thing we want is to go back into the water.

## Everyone Is a Sinner. Without Christ, We Are All the Same

**Romans 3:9 |** "What then? Are we better than they? Not at all. For we have previously charged both Jews and Greeks that they are all under sin."

Paul drove the nail all the way into the wood. "Are we any better?" The answer is a resounding no. There's no place left to stand on religious heritage, circumcision, the Law, or any form of moral superiority. Both Jew and Gentile are under sin. The phrase "under sin" is important. Paul didn't say we've all committed a few sins here and there. He was saying we're all under its power, its grip, its authority, and its curse. We're not dabbling in sin; we're drowning in it and ruled by it.

This is the punchline of the argument Paul was building since the first chapter. And it's meant to leave everyone silenced. No excuses. No comparisons. Just the raw, level ground of human depravity. The moral person doesn't stand any higher than the immoral one. The religious

person doesn't have a cleaner record than the irreligious. In fact, as Paul has already shown, those who claim moral or religious superiority may be the ones who are most blind to their condition.

> **Romans 3:10-18 |** "As it is written: 'There is none righteous, no, not one; There is none who understands; There is none who seeks after God. They have all turned aside; They have together become unprofitable; There is none who does good, no, not one.' 'Their throat is an open tomb; With their tongues they have practiced deceit'; 'The poison of asps is under their lips'; 'Whose mouth is full of cursing and bitterness.' 'Their feet are swift to shed blood; Destruction and misery are in their ways; And the way of peace they have not known.' 'There is no fear of God before their eyes.'"

Paul strung together a litany of Old Testament quotes—stacking Scripture verses upon Scripture verses to make the case airtight. He wasn't exaggerating or editorializing; he was quoting the Jewish Scriptures that his audience would have known by heart. These aren't Paul's opinions. This is God's long-standing testimony about the human heart.

It's a total diagnosis. Look at the body parts mentioned: throat, tongue, lips, mouth, feet, eyes. Paul was painting a picture of sin that touches every part of us—what we say, what we do, where we go, what we see, how we think. Nothing is untouched. Nothing is left clean.

And it's not just about what people do; it's about what they *don't* do. There is none who seeks after God. There is none who does good. That's more than a behavior problem; it's a heart problem. It's a directional

problem. People don't just wander off course; they run in the wrong direction. It's total rebellion.

Lest someone object, "But I've always sought after God," Paul would remind them that if man says one thing and God says another, God is right, and man is lying. Even our seeking, when it exists, is a response to God's initiative. He calls, and we respond—not the other way around.

Paul's goal wasn't to discourage; it's to demolish self-righteousness. He's clearing the table of every excuse, every loophole, every appeal to goodness. And once the table is cleared, there's only one thing left to receive: mercy. Undeserved, unexpected, and absolutely necessary mercy.

> **Romans 3:19–20** | "Now we know that whatever the law says, it says to those who are under the law, that every mouth may be stopped, and all the world may become guilty before God. Therefore by the deeds of the law no flesh will be justified in His sight, for by the law is the knowledge of sin."

Paul ended this entire section with one of the clearest summary statements in all of Scripture: The Law—God's standard, His righteous expectation, His mirror held up to humanity—was never intended to justify us. It was meant to silence us.

That's what Paul said first: "that every mouth may be stopped" (v. 19). That's courtroom language. This is the moment when the accused, having made all their excuses, finally hears the overwhelming evidence and can say no more. The Law was never meant to serve as a podium from which we shout our righteousness. It's the witness that takes the stand and tells the truth about who we really are. And once it speaks, there's nothing left to say.

This is why Paul said, "all the world may become guilty before God" (v. 19). No one slips through the cracks. No one argues their way out. The Law doesn't grade on a curve. It demands perfection and exposes anything less. That's its job.

And just to be sure we don't miss it, Paul repeated the conclusion another way: "By the deeds of the law no flesh will be justified in His sight" (v. 20). If you're trying to earn God's approval by keeping the law, you've misunderstood what the law is for. It's not a ladder that leads to heaven. It's a spotlight that reveals just how far we've fallen.

The law doesn't save us. It *condemns* us. But even in that condemnation, it makes us aware of our need. Paul said, "by the law is the knowledge of sin" (v. 20). It's like a mirror that shows you the dirt on your face. The mirror can't clean you, but it can show you where you need cleansing.

And that is the necessary function of the law. It prepares the way for grace. It helps us finally let go of the illusion that we can save ourselves. Because once we know we're guilty, we're finally ready to hear that God still wants us anyway.

## Judgement Apart from the Law by Faith in Christ

**Romans 3:21 |** "But now the righteousness of God apart from the law is revealed, being witnessed by the Law and the Prophets."

Here comes the pivot. The hinge. The gospel turn. Two words that changes everything: *But now.*

Up to this point, Paul was methodically building a case against humanity. Everyone is under sin. Everyone has fallen short. The Law

hasn't saved anyone; it's just exposed what was already broken. And just when it feels like the weight is too much to bear, Paul opened the door and let in the light.

*But now* a different kind of righteousness has been revealed. A righteousness that isn't earned through the Law. One that isn't based on behavior or ritual or heritage. This is the righteousness of God—*apart from the law*—and it's finally here, standing in the open.

Here's the wild part: It's not brand new. Paul said it was "witnessed by the Law and the Prophets." In other words, this was always the plan. The Old Testament wasn't a failed system. It was a preview. The Law pointed to the need. The prophets pointed to the solution. And now, the solution has a name.

> **Romans 3:22–23 |** "Even the righteousness of God, through faith in Jesus Christ, to all and on all who believe. For there is no difference; for all have sinned and fall short of the glory of God."

Paul cleared up any confusion about where this righteousness comes from—through faith in Jesus Christ. Not faith in general. Not faith in effort or ancestry. Faith in a Person. In Jesus. The Son of God who fulfilled the Law, bore our sin, and made the way home.

And this righteousness is available "to all and on all who believe" (v. 22). That little phrase is more than poetic; it's powerful. It means nobody is left out. It means the same grace that saves the religious leader is available to the thief on the cross. There's no distinction because the problem is universal.

Paul said it flat out: "All have sinned." Not "some." Not "most." All. And what's the result? *We fall short of the glory of God.* Not just His

approval but His glory. The purpose we were made for. The standard we were meant to reflect. And we've all missed it.

That's the great equalizer. Nobody gets to climb up on a moral pedestal. We've all missed the mark. Yet that's not the end of the story, because while all have sinned, all are invited.

**Romans 3:24 |** "Being justified freely by His grace through the redemption that is in Christ Jesus."

The phrase "being justified freely" is an absolute game changer. It may be the most beautifully overlooked phrase in all of Scripture. It may be three words in English but it's two in Greek: *Dikaioumenoi dorean.* It's important to note a couple of things about this word combination. First, *dikaioumenoi* is the present passive participle of *diaioo* , which is to declare "just" or "righteous." But because of its tense, it means that it is continually happening in the present. In other words, Paul was saying that if it's "now"—which is the present—then we are justified. So, is it now? Then we're righteous in the sight of God. It never ends!

Second, the word *dorean* carries the connation of a gift. It's done "freely." So, this phrase could just as easily be translated, "continually declared just or righteous as a gift." As a matter of fact, the Amplified Bible (AMPC) translates these two words as, "[All] are justified and made upright and in right standing with God, freely and gratuitously by His grace." Wow! There simply isn't a way to express how astounding that is!

In two words, Paul moved from the diagnosis of death to the cure. We are *justified freely*—declared right with God, without payment, without merit, without a list of achievements. The only other location this Greek word for "freely" is used in Scripture is when Jesus said, "They

hated Me without a cause" (John 15:25). Just as there was no cause for their hatred toward Jesus, there is no cause for God's mercy. He gave it anyway. And He continues to do so for all of eternity.

How does justification come? Through grace. Through redemption. Through Jesus. Paul stacked these words on purpose. Grace is God's undeserved favor. Redemption is our rescue and release from bondage. Christ Jesus is the One who made it possible.

It's like Paul was trying to make sure nobody walks away thinking they contributed to his or her salvation. No, this is God's work. Start to finish. If this doesn't make you rejoice, I don't know what will! The black and gloomy background that Paul painted was violently interrupted by blinding brilliant light! This is the pivot point of the gospel.

**Romans 3:25-26 |** "Whom God set forth as a propitiation by His blood, through faith, to demonstrate His righteousness, because in His forbearance God had passed over the sins that were previously committed, to demonstrate at the present time His righteousness, that He might be just and the justifier of the one who has faith in Jesus."

This is sacred ground. Paul used a word here that might feel foreign to us: *propitiation.* But to Paul's audience, it would have landed with incredible weight. The Greek word points to the mercy seat—the place in the tabernacle where the high priest would sprinkle blood to atone for the sins of the people. It was the space between God's holiness and man's sin, and it was covered in blood.

Paul was saying that Jesus is our mercy seat. He is the place where wrath is satisfied, judgment is met, and mercy flows. His blood doesn't just cover our sins symbolically; it pays for them entirely.

And this wasn't some reactive plan. Paul said, "God set Him forth" (v. 25). It was God's initiative. God's design. God's choice. And that matters because it means the cross wasn't something Jesus did to make the Father love us. It was something the Father did to show us He already did.

Paul also explained something that often goes unnoticed: Before the cross, God had passed over sins. Not because they didn't matter, but because He was waiting. He was patient. The blood of bulls and goats was never enough to take away sin. It was a placeholder. And now, the true payment has been made.

And here's the stunning conclusion: God remains just. He didn't ignore sin. He didn't lower the bar. The penalty was paid. *And* He becomes the justifier. He declares us righteous without compromising His own holiness. Only God could pull that off. Only God could remain perfectly just and still call broken people like us forgiven.

> **Romans 3:27-28 |** "Where is boasting then? It is excluded. By what law? Of works? No, but by the law of faith. Therefore we conclude that a man is justified by faith apart from the deeds of the law."

Paul didn't let us wander too far into grace without dealing with the implications. If salvation is by faith and not by works, then what happens to boasting? He answered his own question: It's excluded. Not reduced. Not redirected. Not moderated. It's completely shut out.

There's no room left to pat yourself on the back. There's no place for moral pride or spiritual swagger. Because you didn't earn this. You didn't work for it. You didn't qualify. You received it. By faith. And even

that faith wasn't something you drummed up on your own; it was stirred in you by the kindness of God.

So, if you're tempted to make comparisons, if you feel the need to stack your story next to someone else's and feel a little more righteous because of it, Paul said to stop. You're missing the point. Faith puts us all in the same posture—open-handed, undeserving, rescued.

We're justified not because we kept the Law, but because Jesus did. And we're in Him.

**Romans 3:29-30 |** "Or is He the God of the Jews only? Is He not also the God of the Gentiles? Yes, of the Gentiles also, since there is one God who will justify the circumcised by faith and the uncircumcised through faith."

Paul circled back to the heart of his message in this letter: There is no separate plan for Jew and Gentile. There is one God, and one gospel. The same faith that justifies the circumcised (the Jews) is the faith that justifies the uncircumcised (the Gentiles). The Law doesn't divide us anymore. Heritage doesn't create tiers of salvation. There's just Jesus and everyone who believes is welcomed in.

This is what makes the gospel offensive to the proud and beautiful to the humble. You don't get in because you were born into the right family. You don't get in because you've got a clean record. You get in by trusting the only One who does.

And that one God—the God of Abraham, Isaac, and Jacob—is also the God of every tribe, every tongue, every nation. He's not regional. He's not ethnic. He's not tribal. He's the God of all, and He saves all the same way.

> **Romans 3:31 |** "Do we then make void the law through faith? Certainly not! On the contrary, we establish the law."

Paul anticipated one last objection. If faith had replaced Law as the basis of righteousness, does that mean the Law is useless? Is it obsolete? Paul answered again with his familiar phrase: "Certainly not!" That's his way of slamming the door on any idea that faith and law are at odds.

In fact, Paul said the opposite: Faith establishes the law. That sounds like a paradox at first, but it makes perfect sense when you see the full story. Jesus didn't abolish the law, He fulfilled it. Every standard. Every sacrifice. Every shadow in the Old Testament pointed to Him. And when we place our faith in Him, we're saying, "The Law was right. The standard was perfect. I just couldn't meet it, but Jesus did."

So, when we trust Christ, we're not dismissing the Law. We're honoring it more fully than we ever could by trying to obey it on our own. We're saying the :aw was always pointing toward something greater— toward someone greater. And we've found Him.

This is how Paul ended chapter 3. Not with a loophole but with a promise. You don't have to earn your way in. You can't. But the great news is that you don't have to. The door is open. The veil has been torn in two. The blood has been shed. The mercy seat has been made available and you're free to approach by faith.

# Review and Reflection— Romans 3

Let's slow our pace again and let these questions linger. Don't rush past them. Invite them to probe the hidden places of your heart, your thoughts, and even your assumptions about God and yourself. Maybe let them stir up a conversation with a friend over coffee or during your quiet moments with God.

1. **Entrusted, Not Entitled:**

   Paul reminded the Jewish audience that being entrusted with God's word wasn't a badge of superiority; it was a sacred responsibility. Where are you tempted to confuse being entrusted with spiritual privilege as proof of your own righteousness? Where has God entrusted you with His truth, and how are you stewarding that?

   _____

   _____

   _____

2. **Let God Be True, Even When It's Hard:**

   Paul said, "Let God be true and every man a liar" (Romans 3:4). That's a bold, bracing statement. Where do you struggle to let

God's truth overrule your feelings, opinions, or even the loud voices of culture? How might you practice letting God have the final word this week?

_____

_____

_____

3. **Sin as a Perverse Excuse?**

Paul demolished the argument that says, "If my sin makes God look good, why not keep sinning?" Have you ever caught yourself quietly justifying sin because you knew grace would cover it? What would it look like to let God's grace lead you toward holiness, not away from it?

_____

_____

_____

4. **All Have Fallen Short:**

Paul brought us face-to-face with the uncomfortable truth that Jew, Gentile, every person on the planet is under sin. How does that level playing field challenge your thinking about people who seem "worse" or "better" than you? Where might God be inviting you to see others—and yourself—through the lens of grace rather than comparison?

_____

_____

_____

**5. The Mirror, Not the Ladder:**

Paul said the Law isn't a ladder to climb; it's a mirror that shows us our need for rescue. Where are you still trying to climb instead of letting the mirror do its work? Where do you need to stop striving and start trusting?

_____

_____

_____

**6. But Now:**

Those two words—"But now" (Romans 3:21)—mark the turning point of the letter. God's righteousness has been revealed apart from our efforts, through Jesus. How does that reality reframe your story? Where have you been trying to earn what God has already given freely?

_____

_____

_____

**7. The Mercy Seat of Jesus:**

Paul described Jesus as our mercy seat—the place where God's judgment and mercy meet. How does that image stir your heart? What would it look like to live each day remembering that Jesus covers your sin, satisfies the law's demands, and opens the door to the Father?

_____

_____

_____

8. **No More Boasting:**

   Paul finished by silencing all boasting. If salvation is a gift of grace, there's nothing left to brag about except Jesus. Where is God calling you to stop boasting in yourself (even subtly)? How might living from a place of quiet gratitude change the way you approach others, yourself, and even God?

   _____

   _____

   _____

## Heart-Level Reflections

Let these reflections stay with you through the week. Maybe pray them out loud, write them down, or let them become part of your inner conversation with the Lord.

■ **Am I Still Trying to Pay the Debt?**

   Even though I know Jesus paid the ransom, where do I still live as if I owe God something? What would it feel like to stop paying and start praising?

   _____

   _____

   _____

- **Grace as the Engine, Not the Excuse:**

  When I think about grace, do I treat it more like a safety net or the engine of my life? Where might I be using it to excuse sin rather than letting it fuel my transformation?

  _____

  _____

  _____

  _____

- **Letting Go of the Ladder:**

  Where in my faith walk have I built ladders to prove myself to God or others? What would it look like to put down the hammer and nails, and instead stand before God holding only the cross?

  _____

  _____

  _____

  _____

## Prayer Prompts

Let these prayers be more like real conversations—not stiff, not religious. Let them be as raw and real as your heart needs them to be.

- **A Prayer of Gratitude for the Mercy Seat:**

  "Jesus, You are my mercy seat. You took my place. You satisfied every demand the law made against me. I don't want to live one more day as if I'm trying to pay You back. Help me rest in what You've done, and live like someone who is already free."

_____

_____

_____

- **A Prayer to Stop Climbing and Start Trusting:**

  "Father, I've been climbing ladders—trying to prove, trying to perform, trying to be enough. Today, I want to stop. I want to stand at the foot of the cross and let Your love wash over me. Help me believe that 'But now . . .' changes everything."

_____

_____

_____

_____

- **A Prayer to Silence the Boast:**

  "Spirit of God, quiet the voice in me that wants to boast, compare, or climb. Let my only boast be Jesus, and let my life reflect the humility of someone who knows they've been saved by grace alone."

_____

_____

_____

_____

# Action Steps

Again, these aren't checklist tasks. They're invitations to walk out the truths we're discovering together.

1. **Write Out Romans 3:23-24:**

   Put it where you'll see it every day this week. Let it remind you that while all have sinned, the story doesn't end there. Grace has the final word.

   _____

   _____

   _____

   _____

2. **Confess Where You're Still Climbing:**

   Take some time in prayer this week to ask God, "Where am I still trying to earn what You've already given?" When He shows you, confess it and let it go.

   _____

   _____

   _____

   _____

3. **Celebrate Someone Else's Grace Story:**

   Find someone this week whose story of God's grace inspires you. Celebrate it. Encourage them. Let it remind you that you're part of the same grace-filled family.

_____

_____

_____

**4. Stop the Boast Before It Starts:**

The next time you feel the urge to boast, whether about your faith, your discipline, or your spiritual heritage, pause. Instead, turn it into praise for Jesus and His goodness. See how that shifts your heart.

_____

_____

_____

**5. Create a Mercy Seat Moment:**

Set aside some quiet time this week to sit alone with God. Imagine yourself before the mercy seat—Jesus Himself. Let that sacred space remind you that the price is paid, the door is open, and you are welcomed in.

_____

_____

_____

# Closing Thoughts: Where We've Been and Where We're Going

If you've made it this far, you've walked through some of the most humbling—and important—truths ever written. We've looked straight into the mirror Paul held up in Romans 1 through 3, and we've seen what he saw: that all of humanity, from the rebellious to the religious, stands guilty before a holy God. That's not an easy realization to sit with. But it's a necessary one.

We've watched as Paul built an airtight case. He showed us the lostness of those who suppress the truth and chase after their own desires. He called out the hypocrisy of those who judge others while excusing their own failures. And he even challenged the people of Israel—those with the Law and the promises and the pedigree—to recognize that even they fall short. Whether pagan, moralist, or Hebrew, the conclusion is the same: "All have sinned and fall short of the glory of God" (Romans 3:23).

But Paul didn't leave us there. Just when it felt like the weight of that truth might crush us, he opened a window and let grace pour in. He gave us a glimpse of something greater than guilt—a glimpse of *justification*. Not something we could earn, but something offered freely. "Being justified freely by His grace through the redemption that is in Christ Jesus" (Romans 3:24). That one sentence changes everything.

So, where do we go from here?

In the next part of our journey—Narrow Gate Notes on Romans 1-8, Book Two, Chapters 4-8: The Solution We All Need—we're going to explore what this justification actually means for us. We'll hear Paul explain how God's promise has always been based on faith, not works. We'll walk with Abraham and David, watch grace undo what Adam's sin began, and learn what it really means to live in freedom. We'll wrestle with the pull between flesh and spirit, and we'll discover what it looks like to live by the power of the Holy Spirit, fully secure in the love of God.

If Book 1 is about seeing our need for rescue, then Book 2 is about learning how to live as the rescued.

So, take a deep breath. We've laid the foundation. Now it's time to build on it. If the first half of this journey brought conviction, the next half will bring clarity, confidence, and joy.

Let's keep going.

# Endnotes

1. Martin Luther, "Romans 1," Bible Study Tools, 2025. Accessed June 15, 2025. https://www.biblestudytools.com/commentaries/luther/romans/1.html.

2. Jon Courson, 1993 sermon on Romans 2. www. https://www.jon-courson.com/playteaching/w614.

# Let's Connect

Narrow Gate is a place where young men can quiet the distractions of everyday life and discover a life that matters, but it's also a community where people of all ages find purpose in supporting the mission of the organization.

Consider this your invitation to be a part of our family. Whether you're a young man who is considering becoming a student or a friend or family member who knows someone who would benefit from this experience, we invite you to:

- Follow us on Instagram @narrowgatelodge
- Follow us on Facebook @narrowgatefoundation
- Subscribe to our YouTube channel at Narrow Gate Foundation
- Shop our goods made for life at narrowgateleather.org
- Purchase our specialty fresh roast at narrowgate.coffee
- Help transform lives by transforming your home with our real wood beams, mantels, floating shelves and more at tnboxbeams.com
- Sign up for our email newsletters, request a Narrow Gate speaker, schedule a tour, or connect with our staff at info@narrowgate.org or 931-583-0633.

The eight-month residential experience at Narrow Gate Lodge is available to qualified young men, regardless of their financial resources. We have been able to offer students tuition-free experiences since our inception because of the generosity of thousands of people—and we invite you to join us. Narrow Gate is a 501(c)(3) nonprofit and donations are tax deductible.

Would you or your organization like to make a contribution or receive additional information?

Please contact us at:

**931-583-0633**
**office@narrowgate.org**
**P.O. Box 267, Duck River, TN 38454**

Are you a young man between the ages of 18 and 25 who would like to apply?

Learn more at:

**nglodge.org**